The Secret World of the
Working Mother

The Secret World of the
Working
Mother

Juggling Work, Kids and Sanity

Fiona Millar

Vermilion
LONDON

3 5 7 9 10 8 6 4 2

Published in 2009 by Vermilion, an imprint of Ebury Publishing

Ebury Publishing is a Random House Group company

Copyright © Fiona Millar 2009

Fiona Millar has asserted her right to be identified as the author of this Work
in accordance with the Copyright, Designs and Patents Act 1988.

The Random House Group Limited Reg. No. 954009

Addresses for companies within the Random House Group can be found at
www.rbooks.co.uk

A CIP catalogue record for this book is available from the British Library

The Random House Group Limited supports The Forest Stewardship
Council (FSC), the leading international forest certification organisation.
All our titles that are printed on Greenpeace approved FSC certified paper
carry the FSC logo. Our paper procurement policy can be found
at www.rbooks.co.uk/environment

Mixed Sources
Product group from well-managed
forests and other controlled sources
www.fsc.org Cert no. TT-COC-2139
© 1996 Forest Stewardship Council

Printed and bound in Great Britain by Clays of St Ives PLC

Designed and typeset by seagulls.net

ISBN 9780091924232

Copies are available at special rates for bulk orders. Contact the sales
development team on 020 7840 8487 for more information.

To buy books by your favourite authors and register for offers, visit
www.rbooks.co.uk

*This book is dedicated to Audrey,
my own mother, for being such a great role model.*

Contents

Acknowledgements

Thanks are due to Clare Hulton, Hannah MacDonald and everyone at Ebury for their honesty and guidance throughout the writing and publication of this book, to Jonny Geller and Karen Mattison for nudging me into it in the first place, and to Helen Cooper, and everyone at Women Like Us, for helping me track down so many interesting mothers to interview. Some of the interviewees' names have been changed to preserve their privacy but each of their stories touched a nerve and I am indebted to them all.

Sebastian Kraemer, Jessica James, John Coleman, Leon Feinstein, Melissa Benn, Mary Macleod, Jane Roberts, Negley Harte, Kay Carberry, Frances O'Grady, Sarah Veale, Sarah Jackson and Helen Reardon Bond provided invaluable advice and good sense. I am extremely grateful to Zoe Richardson and Mona Ragheb, both still students, for transcribing the interviews and taking such an interest in issues that are yet to touch their lives. I would also like to pay tribute to all the tireless campaigners who keep up the pressure for more progressive policies for working families. Don't give up.

My own children Rory, Calum and Grace have proved to be challenging, wise and incredibly good-natured about their parents' often frenetic lifestyles. My conversations with them have sustained me while writing this book. Love and thanks also go to Alastair for his support and encouragement, for being a wonderful father and for finally accepting that most women do two jobs.

Introduction

Flicking through the papers on the day my second son left home for university, I was struck by a headline 'Late for work? Don't mention the nanny'.

These days I tend to skim over stories about work-life balance. With two children at university, one teenager at home and no nanny, I count myself lucky only to have to worry about who walks the dog.

Even so the 'Don't mention the nanny' story, which claimed that more than half of all working mothers will lie about why they are late for work rather than admit it is because of the kids, triggered an instant and depressing sense of déjà vu.

It is twenty years since I took the plunge and went back to work as a full-time political reporter on a national newspaper, leaving a twelve-week-old baby at home with a young, relatively inexperienced nanny. I can't remember much I enjoyed about the subsequent nine months. I had got pregnant unexpectedly, just after taking on a new job as a lobby correspondent based at the

House of Commons and went back to work full of the best intentions to stick with a job that involved long hours and late nights
when Parliament was sitting. For the remainder of those late
nights, I spent hours feeding the baby I felt so guilty about
leaving during the day.

My son seemed quite happy to be shared out between grandparents, a part-time nanny, and two parents who worked different
shifts on different papers and had one day a week together as a
family. But after nine months of exhaustion, on and off illness, tears
in the ladies' loo in the Commons press gallery (hearing the baby
howling at the other end of the phone), I reached a tipping point one
evening when I got home to find my son reaching out to his grand-
father rather than me. Rightly or wrongly, I decided it was time to
give up work.

Although I didn't realise it then, that was the start of a twenty-
year experiment with every different type of working arrangement
possible. As a couple we made a conscious decision that I would
take on the lion's share of the caring responsibilities, a decision I
have questioned on many occasions since. In the intervening years
I have worked full-time, part-time, flexibly, been a freelance and
done a job-share in my quest to try and do justice to my children,
my education, my training and ambition.

I was lucky in one respect: my original employers at the *Daily
Express*, in spite of being part of what was in every other respect a
very male and socially conservative institution, turned out to be
rather liberated men who went to great lengths to accommodate my
changed circumstances. After the briefest of career breaks they
invited me back with the lure of being able to tailor my working
hours to suit the family, even though it effectively stuffed any chance

of promotion. I juggled various different news desk jobs, several years' freelancing at home and then a part-time feature writer's job with the birth of two more children.

When Alastair took a job as press secretary to the then leader of the Opposition, Tony Blair, a ten-year roller coaster of general elections, his and hers jobs at Downing Street, dramatic and traumatic personal and professional highs and lows followed until we both left the government in 2003.

Throughout it all I have had crashes of confidence, been permanently exhausted, and moderated every career choice with the anxiety that I would let my children down in some way. I have had pangs of regret seeing contemporaries reach the top in their chosen professions and acquire the status and money that goes with it, either because they have chosen not to have a family, or because they somehow managed that delicate emotional balance between work and family better than I did. I am conscious that I have on many occasions traded professional fulfilment, responsibility and status against the competing desire to be a good parent and fulfil the maternal urge, to see my children leave for school in the morning and be able to get back in time for the school assembly or the doctor's appointment if necessary. I have raged against the unfairness of it all but probably wouldn't have had it any other way.

In that period I have been lulled into a sense that much progress has been made in the area of work-life balance and that the prospects for young mothers today have improved. Even though my tabloid newspaper bosses turned out to be quite progressive blokes when it came to keeping women in work, I was acutely aware in the late Eighties that not all my friends and contemporaries were as lucky as I was when they tried to go back to work after having babies. For many of them it was a choice of working or not working. The options of returning were usually limited by the fact that the costs of childcare outweighed an average salary. Many women were faced with the blunt choice that they were going back to work for the sake of it, for self esteem, or in some cases because they were honest enough to admit that being at home with the kids all day drove them mad.

Either way it was tough call. But twenty years later, with the equal opportunities and sex discrimination legislation of the Seventies firmly embedded, recent progress on maternity leave, a new awareness of the need for employers to be at least seen to be family friendly and the promise of massive state investment in high-quality nursery care, it should be much simpler. Girls are storming through the education system, account for a large part of the expansion in university places and are doing so because they have aspirations to be independent and fulfilled. Around three-quarters of families have two working parents. The one-and-a-half bread-winner model of the 'average family' suggests that most families need more than one income. Women's prospects at work will undoubtedly be affected by a downturn in the economy but the long term trend of women returning to work after childbirth is unlikely to shift.

More than two-thirds of working-age women with dependent children are now working (compared to 90 per cent of men). But the stereotypical image of the power-suited women, complete with big shoulder pads, 'having it all', was always something of a myth, perpetuated by the newspapers in which many of those women worked.

The new generation of working mothers who account for the

dramatic increase in women's employment over the past thirty years are often balancing work relationships, home life and children by working part-time, or flexibly. Increasing numbers even set up as entrepreneurs, from home, as a route into more manageable working patterns if their employers are not receptive to the idea of them working part-time or organising working hours to suit school-age children. That determination to find ways of making employment work for them has also been balanced by a growing willingness, and even enthusiasm, among many younger fathers to take part in their children's care, even if they are less prepared to share some of the domestic chores and work flexibly themselves. Almost 40 per cent of women with dependent children work part-time, compared to 4 per cent of men with the same family responsibilities. Women still do on average three-quarters of domestic 'housework' hours and the increase in women's paid work has not been matched by an equivalent increase in men's unpaid work in the home.

And that, in turn, has led to worrying ongoing inequalities for mothers returning to work. Losing work experience and chopping and changing part-time jobs only amplifies the pay gap, reduces opportunities for promotion and partially contributes to the ongoing 'occupational segregation' that has bedevilled the British workplace for generations and locks thousands of women into lower-status, more poorly paid jobs than their husbands, partners and male friends. Even though the numbers of women in high status establishment jobs like the judiciary, politics and business are creeping up, women are still woefully underrepresented in top jobs. Only 11 per cent of directors at the FTSE top one hundred companies are women.

Much of the inspiration for the book came from meeting Karen Mattison and Emma Stewart, who founded a social enterprise called Women Like Us.

Women Like Us is based on the brilliant but simple idea of using the school gate, the place where most mothers tend to congregate, as a forum to link women up to jobs which match the hours and patterns they want to work.

It is also an organisation which recognises that the journey back to work, for many women, is not just solved by the practical business of finding a job but needs to be accompanied by emotional and psychological support, which no woman should feel ashamed of for needing.

Too many women still give up careers for which they are well trained and qualified when they have children and eventually go back to lower-status jobs simply to balance home and work. Often the birth of subsequent children means their work lives are regularly interrupted, with their chances of getting back on the career ladder fatally wounded.

Much of the evidence, both polling and anecdotal, suggests that even though the political climate has changed, with government policies more actively supportive of working mothers and the nuts and bolts of organising work versus family life improving gradually, the culture within many workplaces has not.

During the interviews for this book I was initially shocked, but increasingly unsurprised, to hear stories about women who felt they did have to lie to their employers to cover for a child's illness, or women who faced bullying and low-level intimidation when they returned to work after childbirth.

I laugh now when I retell the story of how I allowed my two-

year-old son to cut his way through his sweatshirt (which he was
wearing at the time) with a pair of sharp scissors while I spoke on
the telephone to a (female) editor for whom I was working. At the
time the sense of horror I felt about what I was allowing him to do
was overridden by an equally strong urge not to acknowledge that
I was both working and caring for a small child, a dual role, which
at the time seemed to be the ultimate cop-out. The fact that mothers still lack the confidence to affirm that parenthood has equal
status with work is depressing.

The transition from being a childless working woman to a
mother going back to work can be a difficult, even traumatic,
process. It throws up complex issues, not just about finding the
right job and dealing with the emotional wrench of leaving a small
baby, but also about ambition, aspiration, confidence and self-
esteem and identity.

Women's identities are shaped by the choices they make yet
we are often also haunted by the choices we have not made,
fantasising about how green the grass is on the other side. For every
woman who secretly feels she is a poor role model because she
doesn't work and who dreads the question 'So what do you do?'
from the casual (usually male) acquaintance – in case the eyes glaze
over when you explain that you a) do nothing, b) look after the
kids, c) work part-time, d) a combination of all three – there will
be another who can give an arresting answer but may be secretly
worried that the reason her child is naughty or falling behind at
school is because she is at work.

Managing that cocktail of emotional and psychological reactions
to motherhood and work, as well as relationships with partners,
colleagues and your children's carers in the privacy of your own

home is hard enough. In a hostile working environment, the decision to resume a career or take a new job can quickly seem catastrophic. In the company of friends, some of whom may have chosen different paths post childbirth, it can also bring challenges. Yet a decision to quit can often lead to a period out of work, a crash in confidence and a de-skilling in the rapidly changing world of technology which only compounds the difficulties of resuming a career, or taking up a different, more flexible job later, when the reality gradually dawns that children grow up, become more independent and no longer need you 24/7 ... something no one ever warns you about when they are tiny.

The women interviewed for this book are from a wide range of backgrounds and parts of the country, randomly selected but representative of many types of work-life balance situations. They disprove the glib generalisations and scare stories about working mothers which, in the last few years alone, have ranged from the ongoing promotion of the idea that you can be superwoman and 'have it all' to claims that working mothers are responsible for giving themselves breast cancer, and are likely to have delinquent, low-achieving, often obese, children.

The stories of the women in this book weave a complex narrative that reminds us that both work and parenting are a continuum, with good and bad bits on the way; once women have children, they make many more changes in their working lives than men ever do, and these can lead to inspiring achievements as well as 'occupational downgrading'. Whether, then, a pattern is a vicious or virtuous cycle depends on so many other factors: the type of child they have, the quality of the childcare, their relationship with their partner, their employer, and the support they can count on from family and friends in their local community. The usual image of a working mother is that of a woman separated from a small baby. But our children grow up, and working can bring different pressures to bear on the parents of teenagers, especially in an age where parents are held responsible for their children's achievement, behaviour and happiness and publicly blamed for failing to guarantee it.

There is no right or wrong way to combine work and motherhood. Every story allows us to glimpse what goes on in the secret world of individual women and families and will show that, if you can get all the ingredients right, balancing home and work is not an impossible dream. This book will chart a path of how it can be done, from the moment when you decide whether or not you want to go back to work and have to contemplate the reality of being parted from your new baby, through possible changes to your working arrangements, the childcare maze of children's centres, round-the-clock provision, private nurseries, workplace nurseries, nannies, childminders, friends and family, after-school clubs and extended schools.

What happens if you begin to realise that it may not be working for you? How easy is it to leave and then face re-entry to the world of work after a long break; to rebuild confidence; how do you work out if you really want to do something different and then develop the skills and confidence to make a change? And what happens to the dynamic within the home as the power balance shifts between two individuals working full-time with roughly equal status to a couple in which one partner works full-time and the other part-time, or not at all?

Then there is the expectation that life will get simpler as the children get older. I found myself agreeing with many of the women interviewed in this book who spoke of a relatively golden period when children are in the later stages of primary school and it appears that you have cracked the work-life balance game.

However, the onset of adolescence in a child who has until that point been biddable, loving and companionable, can then plunge you into a phase of parenting that no one and few handbooks prepare us for. It is hard to find a carer for a teenager and even harder to keep on top of the never-ending round of tests, exams and coursework that schools impose. Is there any easy answer to managing that phase of working parenthood?

Years ago, in one of my most stressful periods of managing work and home – which involved co-authoring a book, moving house, working part-time and managing a freelance career from home with two small children and a part-time nanny – I interviewed the former Health Secretary and the then director of the Institute of Public Policy Research, Patricia Hewitt, about the issues facing women at the time. She told me that she was the only girl in her primary school whose mother had worked; that her mother was always doing two or three things at once and used to quote the line from Rudyard Kipling's poem 'If' about 'the unforgiving minute' to her children.

If you can fill the unforgiving minute
With sixty seconds' worth of distance run
Yours is the Earth and everything that's in it
And – which is more – you'll be a Man, my son!

That phrase 'the unforgiving minute' has haunted me ever since, usually cursed as I start sorting washing at 11pm, try and put my make-up on in the car or, as I used to do, dive into an equally unforgiving swimming pool at six in the morning to allow myself an hour of contemplation and exercise before the kids got up for school. A battle with time is the constant backdrop to the lives of so many modern mothers and hearing how other women cope, deal with stress, make time for themselves, chill out, find the energy to think through their work-life balance problems and still maintain the resilience and aspiration to move forward will, I hope, play an inspiring and simple part in resolving our own personal dilemmas.

CHAPTER 1

The Invisible Umbilical Cord

One of my most treasured possessions from my pre-baby days is a cartoon drawn by one of my then colleagues from the daily paper on which I worked when, at twenty-nine, I unexpectedly got pregnant. In it I am shown resplendently expectant, with hair flowing and smiling cheerily as I depart on maternity leave as others raise a glass to my good health, the baby and our future. It always makes me smile now. I can remember so clearly the day I received it, leaving work convinced that within months I would be back at my desk, clad in my power suit, figure back in place, and probably sharing a drink with the same gang at the end of the day. I think, although it is hard to remember, that in my projected future life, the baby was a much-loved but compliant creature who would be dutifully ensconced somewhere with the nanny we hadn't yet employed, while my life carried on basically as before.

The possibility of *not* going back to work *never* crossed my mind. I had five months off on full pay which, compared to many friends and relatives, felt generous and empowering and surely the basis to storm back to work with a baby under my belt and continue climbing the career ladder? I had just been promoted to the political team at Westminster and the future seemed bright. Two months later, having lost a substantial chunk of that valuable post-maternity period because my son was literally dragged into the world with forceps almost three weeks late, I had morphed into a different creature altogether.

The woman who used to get up every morning at the crack of dawn to swim before working an eight- to ten-hour day was replaced by someone who often forgot to get dressed before early afternoon. I was blissfully happy and the baby was as envis-aged, adorable and easy, although it is very hard at that stage to grasp that babies can and do change. Little did I realise, for example, that he would start waking four or five times in the night shortly after I returned to work when he was twelve weeks old. In the dim, dark hours of the night this always struck me as being his way of clawing back the time with me that he was missing during the day. I sometimes wonder whether I would have viewed my return to work with such equanimity if he had been less settled and easy going.

Since then I have lost count of the number of times that I have heard younger friends and colleagues tell me authoritatively, as they approach the end of their pregnancies, that they too will of course be returning to work. I find myself wondering whether they will, gently suggesting that they might feel differently after the baby but equally conscious that until you have given birth it is impossible to comprehend the physical, emotional and psychological changes that follow.

I wish I had known then what I know now; that what will

follow will be not only months of physical recovery, exhaustion, wonder and tears, quite likely accompanied by the realisation that what appeared to be a relationship of two equals with your baby's father is now hopelessly unbalanced, and other relationships with family and friends are thrown out of kilter, but also that your identity is suddenly split between 'independent working woman' and 'full-time carer' – and that a new cloak of expectations descends from the outside world.

Now, more than ever, parenting is seen as a cross between a job and a high-octane leisure activity. Newspapers and magazines devote sections to family and parenting alongside traditional gardening, cooking and property topics, politicians express subtle but menacing warnings about penalties that will befall 'bad' parents, leaving us in no doubt that we are expected to care for and steer our children through to well-rounded adulthood, hoovering up armfuls of GCSEs and A-levels in the process, while also continuing to work, so we don't cost the state money either in welfare payments or in terms of lost national income.

The fact that women tend to choose either more flexible work after they have children, lose work experience and then subsequently trade down to less prestigious or high-earning jobs or give up completely has been estimated to cost the national economy between £15 billion and £23 billion a year. Society has high expectations of us as workers and mothers and few would now *publicly* question women's right or desire to work once they have had children in the way that they might have done only forty or fifty years ago. But there is still a great deal of barely hidden ambivalence about mothers which expresses itself in the public exhortations for us to be better parents, and in a stream of often conflicting stories in the media implying that there really is an ineradicable contradiction between the good mother and the working woman.

In one cursory search of the Internet I found a handful of stories which categorically stated that middle-class mothers – middle class being the code for working, even though working-class mothers have genuinely worked since the year dot – risked giving themselves breast cancer by giving up breastfeeding too soon, delaying motherhood or doing stressful jobs; risked their children becoming unhealthy and obese because they were too busy to prepare nutritious food; jeopardised their children's chances of success at school and increased their risk of becoming delinquents (or even put their lives at risk) by farming them out to inadequate carers. Following the – statistically, highly unusual – example of an assault on a child by her childminder, the commentator Minette Marrin wrote, in an article headlined 'Pushing mothers back into work is wrong': 'You leave your babies and little children with childminders and crèche workers at great risk – to them, to yourself and to society at large.'

Usually the screaming headlines are based on reports or academic research which are much more balanced. Often a general 'rule' is based on the fact that very small numbers of children experience negative outcomes when their mothers work. However, there is no getting away from the gnawing doubts that spring from a slow drip-drip of negative opinion, especially when they trickle down into the views of friends and family.

Over the years my own mother has been the person who most typifies the ambivalence that still exists about working mothers; she is also the one person whose criticism hurts the most and who can most successfully hold up a mirror to my own anxieties. From a working-class background and having left school herself at fifteen, she went back to studying in the post-war years and ended up re-training as a teacher in her forties. She worked on and off during our childhood and my less-than-cooperative teenage years, nudged and cajoled me on to university, understandably taking huge pride in my degree and subsequent journalistic career until I had the children when her more frequent refrain became, 'You are doing too much ... what about the children?' Comments which, I gradually noted, were never aimed either at her equally hard-working son, or my children's father.

None of this will even be part of the background noise when you are lying in your hospital bed enjoying your first cup of post-natal weak tea and toast. In the weeks and months to come the realisation will slowly dawn that being a mother in the 21st century involves managing conflict, just as it always did.

The working mother may appear to have been a new phenom-enon, bred in our lifetimes and epitomised in the Eighties and Nineties by the 'have-it-alls', led by commanders-in-chief Margaret Thatcher and city high-flyer and mother-of-six Nicola Horlick, but women have always worked.

There may have been regional and class-based differences in how and where they worked but in pre-industrial Britain women worked steadily in agriculture, retail, domestic service, they worked in the home as spinners, dressmakers, embroiderers, straw plaiters and lace-makers. They also worked with their children – the 'spinning jenny' was originally designed for a young teenage girl – and children often travelled around the country with their 'working mothers'.

The historian Pamela Sharpe's accounts of working women in Essex in the 18th century shows their early entrepreneurial skills;

women traded in everything from agricultural produce, cooked food to haberdashery, often travelling huge distances to make ends meet if they were widowed or had an absent partner. One example of an early female entrepreneur was Ann Hart who became a pedlar in 1761 when her husband went into the navy. She and her youngest child were supported by 'buying and selling blue rags and such pedlary wares about ye country'.

As industrialisation progressed the preferred role for the aspirant middle-class female was one of homemaker, good mother and creator of the Victorian domestic idyll. The better-off continued to farm their children out to nurses and governesses, men dominated the public sphere, but working-class women continued to supplement the family income by labouring in the home, small workshops or factories. Oral histories of that time confirm the hard grind of working in an era before domestic appliances shored up our domestic lives.

Economic historian Elizabeth Roberts's book *A Woman's Place*, compiled from interviews with working families in the North-West between 1890 and 1940, paints a vivid picture of families where both parents worked out of sheer financial necessity. Their lives, she writes, were 'stressful and demanding in the extreme' and a common refrain was that they were made up of 'bed and work'. Housework had to be fitted in first thing in the morning and at the weekends. One interviewee, whose mother was a weaver and father a labourer, wondered that her mother's prodigious energy even extended to baking bread late at night.

'She used to get up at 5.45 to have a drink of tea and take a sandwich. You prepared at night for the following morning. It was always a question of you washed yourself, you looked at the buttons, and there was a row if you wanted a button at the last minute. You cleaned your clogs, you put them there and you went to bed. Then everything was ready for the morning; they all did the same. Then off to work … it was bed and work all the time in those days.'

Another described her mother starting her domestic chores at six in the evening after work: 'They didn't have gas in the kitchen so they had to do the washing with the great big mangle with two candles on top. That was starting at six o'clock and baking and washing. There had to be so much done each night. It was at week-ends mostly when everything was bottomed. It was hard work, it was all bed and work … washing and cooking and things like that during the week, tidying and dusting, but Saturday and Sunday was the main days for a good clean-up.'

Children were usually 'minded' by other women – a relative or neighbour as formal full-time child-minding arrangements could be costly; part-time unpaid arrangements with friends and family appear to be common. One couple employed in the cotton industry in the 1930s paid their son's aunt ten shillings a week to mind him. As the husband explained: 'You only got paid for what you produced. I know it happened one week, the wage was 18s and she had to pay her sister so she had worked all week for 8s.'

Nothing changes then. Census figures over the last two centuries show that women's employment rates were fairly constant throughout the mid-Victorian era when around 40 per cent of all women worked. They reached a low point in the late 19th century when around a third of all adult women worked. During the two world wars the number of women in work shot up. During the First World War an estimated two million women filled the jobs left vacant by men fighting at the front and by 1943 over 80 per cent of women were involved in the Second World War effort in some way. But they were jobs that quickly slipped away once the servicemen returned. By 1951, 43 per cent of working-age women were in employment but the next half-century saw a transformation in the women's labour market and today around 75 per cent of working-age women have jobs. In the same period much has changed both culturally and in terms of legal rights.

The early hardline feminism of the Sixties and Seventies, which often appeared to condemn women for wanting to be with their children and viewed motherhood as a feeble excuse for not wanting to compete on rigidly equal terms with men, gradually gave way to a new, more malleable version – how to manage the balance between work and home once the novelty of the supermum began to wear off. Women started to feel it was OK to admit to being exhausted, demoralised and often isolated by the constant juggling, especially if they were dealing with intransigent, unsympathetic employers. In 1988, the year I returned to work, the now-defunct Maternity Alliance produced a pamphlet based on interviews with several hundred women who were going back to work for the first time, to hear from real women what it was like.

Only a tiny minority reported being offered any phased or structured return to work and several talked openly about their emotional turmoil. One woman employed by the BBC said: 'Having spent twenty-nine weeks with my baby in my arms most of the day, ten and a half hours without holding him was dreadful. I felt like snatching passing babies from pushchairs just for a cuddle.'

While many of the interviewees reported feeling well supported by their immediate workmates and were often welcomed back with flowers and cards, especially from female colleagues with children, many also talked of the underlying assumptions they met from others in their workplaces about what a woman's correct role in life should be. Some faced outright hostility.

Over a third described the reaction of their bosses as hostile – one woman reported her supervisor's welcome-back message as: 'You've had a nice rest over the last few months, now it is time to do some work' – or sadly indifferent. A woman college lecturer in London felt intense disappointment that none of her colleagues seemed interested in her baby: 'I took some photos in with me but the opportunity to show them never seemed to arise. They came home unopened. The canteen staff have shown most interest in her and ask about her frequently.'

Books like Maeve Haran's *Having It All* in 1991, about the TV executive who chucks in the life of a high-powered working mother, and Allison Pearson's *I Don't Know How She Does It*, ten years later and dubbed by one reviewer as 'the national anthem for working mums', caught the public's imagination.

Both focused on the dilemmas for the full-time high-powered working mum. Even though she has always been in a minority, since the rapid increase in women's employment in the last fifty years has been almost exclusively made up by part-time jobs, the full-time working mother has always been disproportionately represented in the media where the few women executives who do shatter the glass ceiling tend to work full-time.

Yet the trials and tribulations of Pearson's hedge-fund manager Kate Reddy, who juggled work and home and battered shop-bought mince pies in the small hours to give them the home-cooked look for the next day's school event, contained grains of truth about so many of our lives and somehow reinforced the view that being a full-time working mother might not be a realistic aspiration after all.

Women's magazines in the early Nineties were aimed at working women, the then newly relaunched *She* magazine ('for women who juggle their lives') attracting particular interest when editor Linda Kelsey, herself a full-time working mother, left her job. She subsequently wrote that for working mums, Helen Gurley Brown's famous catchphrase 'Having it all' needed a rewrite. Doing it all was more like it. By the late 1990s, a new honesty was emerging about how difficult it was when women who had been educated with a view to a career came head to head with being a parent.

In her book *Madonna and Child* the writer Melissa Benn described the difficulties of facing what she called the pressures of 'premature returnism'. Even in the new, more honest, climate of the later-wave feminism, the urge for professional women to show that motherhood hadn't changed them and that they could have it all was still conflicting:

'As the new mother of a young child and as a self-employed writer, I had been back at work, if fitfully, within weeks of the birth, resentfully taking transatlantic calls at some unearthly hour of the night on an article that needed more work on it. This was at a time when all I wanted to do was gaze at my new baby girl and not worry about money or the outside world, or whether I was still considered a serious person.'

The importance of being able to spend those first few months gazing at your baby, watching his or her development and laying the foundations for a relationship that needs to last a lifetime have since been recognised in the legal rights that new mothers can enjoy. Most women are now entitled to take six months off work, with an option to extend that depending on how long they have been in their jobs. Fathers also have the right to paid leave to support their post-natal partners. Six months is significant as it coincides with the time when the baby's world is starting to change quite rapidly. He or she can sit up, start to enjoy relationships with a wider circle of family, siblings, grandparents and other carers. The separation anxiety hasn't quite started to set in, so it can often feel like the right moment to go back to work.

The government's own research suggests that too many women still don't take their full leave entitlement because they receive only the state maternity pay, and do not have the benefit of extra 'occupational' maternity pay that some public and private sector companies offer. Many women also don't realise that they might be entitled to take off more than six months.

The practical and legal context in which women now return to work may be improving but no one can legislate for the emotions that can loom large over leaving your baby for the first time whether he or she is three, six or twelve months old. Some women can just walk out the door and not look back. Others can have the best maternity deal in the world, the most sympathetic employer, supportive husband or partner and an army of nannies and grannies, yet still find themselves struggling to slip those invisible ties that pull in the opposite direction as they set off for work; especially tough if you have to shut the front door on a howling child.

From the sleepy east-coast village where she now lives and runs her own small business making curtains, Angela appears quietly confident and comfortable with the choices she has made since the first of her two daughters was born more than ten years ago. The girls, Sadie and Evie, are both settled in primary and secondary schools, and Angela has an enviable lifestyle which allows her to spend time with them after school, run her business – which she is now contemplating expanding to employ more people – and also indulge her passions for riding and tap dancing, both of which she does locally. Her work-life balance is so well tuned that she can even run down to the stables to let off steam if the pressure of work becomes too great.

However, the inner turmoil she experienced in the first year of motherhood is still keenly felt. In spite of having a job she loved and that gave her the intellectual challenge she wanted, as a biologist working for a boss who was responsive and sensitive to the fact that she was a new mum, the pain and anxiety of being separated from her baby proved overwhelming.

Her husband had just been made redundant and was in the process of setting up his own IT company when the baby arrived. The house they had bought on the outskirts of Oxford gave her the luxury of a ten-minute walk to work, but the size of the mortgage also meant she had no choice but to return. Her fear about leaving Sadie set in early on.

'We went to a restaurant and she was about four weeks old then,' Angela says. 'I was breastfeeding and had left her with a babysitter who we knew and all I can remember is just desperately wanting to go back home. My husband couldn't understand it and I'll always remember that because it was so distressing for me.'

Angela eventually went back to work full-time when the baby was around four months old.

'I hadn't stopped breastfeeding but I still didn't feel quite as bad about the separation before I went back to work because I knew we needed the money. The firm I worked for had never had someone off pregnant before so they had very basic maternity standards and I couldn't stay off for longer.'

For many women like Angela, the anxieties over separation are wrapped up in a complex mix of other emotions, not least about the substitute carer: Angela and her husband had wanted a nursery place for their baby daughter but demand for nursery places locally was high, with long waiting lists, so they hired a nanny. Even though her husband was working at home setting up his new business he needed to be able to travel at short notice so couldn't be relied on for childcare.

'I've kicked myself since then that we only ever interviewed the one person. I was so pleased to get someone because we left it a bit late, to be honest; as soon as she started I wasn't happy with her. I think that was mainly because I didn't want her looking after my daughter. I remember feeding the baby in the morning but because our house was terraced with one of those paths down the side, I could hear the gates go and I would think "She is here now, I don't even want her to come into the house". I just wished I could be staying there to look after her.'

Angela's boss wasn't just supportive of her return to work – she describes him as a committed 'family man' who allowed her to work her basic hours, didn't put pressure on her to stay late, was understanding when her daughter was sick – but he also went out of his way to ensure she got job satisfaction by promoting her in her first year back. When there were busy periods in the office and she sensed that some of her colleagues were frustrated or raising their eyebrows at her determination to leave work on time, he always 'put them straight'.

'He was brilliant and told them that they did their hours and

I did mine and if they needed extra help they should go and find it elsewhere. I don't think I could have asked any more of the company.'

However the fact that the office was within walking distance of home made it even harder to let go and Angela would find herself being drawn back home at lunchtime simply to catch a glimpse of her daughter.

'I would come home and this nanny would be sitting there and my husband would be in his office which I thought felt really odd. Then at the end of the day I would leave work straight away, I never used to hang around. I just wasn't coping very well at all. I just wanted to be at home and hated coming back and seeing another woman in my house looking after my baby ... I just didn't want her to be there.'

Eventually they found a nursery for the baby which was expensive but, from Angela's point of view, money well spent: 'I was happier that we didn't have the nanny and that this other woman wasn't in my house looking after my child because it felt like I was an outsider. But I still felt that pull. I still felt at half-past five that I couldn't wait to get out. She was my daughter and I had to go and get her. That pull. It never stopped actually.'

Angela's gut-level anxiety about leaving her baby will be familiar to many women; it is almost like an invisible umbilical cord is being stretched and pulling you back home when your work commitments are pulling you away. Often it is accompanied by fears that are almost too irrational to share: what if the baby really does start to love someone else more than you; what if the nursery carers are cruel and neglectful; what if the children go out on a trip and get crushed by a car; or if the house goes up in flames?

Even when our older children were toddlers and I had a part-time job as a feature writer on a national newspaper, I can remember the irrational but nonetheless genuine sense of panic I felt when their nanny, who I trusted implicitly and was in fact more responsible and organised with the children than I could ever be, wanted to take them to the seaside for the day. It was almost as if I had drawn an imaginary geographical boundary around myself which included our home, that allowed me to feel secure if they were within it but exposed if they moved too far away. Dropping them off at Victoria Station that day was agonising and seemed unbelievably foolish when they subsequently returned home intact and, of course, happy to have had the sort of day out with a bucket and spade that would have been hard to find in London.

Magazine editor Dee had her first daughter when she was eighteen, having left her inner-London secondary school without any qualifications. Two more children followed in the next five years and she stayed at home until they were all at nursery and school, when she started working again (initially as a bus driver), which was the start of a process that took her to college, university and eventually into work as a professional journalist. Her three older children were in their teens by the time she remarried and had her fourth child, and the family was living in the London suburbs with considerable financial commitments which meant that Dee went back to work very soon after her youngest daughter Rachel's birth.

As an experienced older mum the strain of the early separation from her daughter proved doubly shocking. 'That was probably the most difficult thing that I've ever had to do. I hadn't gone back when my others were so young but I had to go back to work when she was four months old, partly for financial reasons – my husband had just started a business so we were waiting for it to develop – but also because I hadn't been in my job for very long.

'So there was quite a lot of pressure on me at that time. I had a childminder, luckily someone that went to the same church that I went to. But it was still horrible. I remember walking into the London Underground interchange between Bank, the Central line and the District line and feeling this milk welling up inside me. It was almost like mourning, because I had been with her for four months and the separation was traumatic, really difficult. I am glad the law has changed now. There are still many other women who will always be in that position but if you can avoid it, avoid it.'

The sense of loss, anxiety and the desire to return to the yearned-for baby are mixed up with guilt feelings over whether they are missing us, or whether we are indeed being 'good enough' mothers. Of course it is perfectly natural for children to miss their parents when they are apart from them, and the chances are that once you get to work, and get distracted, the immediate trauma of separation will fade away. The question many mothers wrestle with is whether that loss and separation is damaging to the baby in the longer term.

For much of the 20th century the notion of the 'good mother' was linked to the work of John Bowlby, the London-born child psychiatrist, whose 'attachment theory' overshadowed thinking about mother-child relationships. Born in a classic Edwardian upper middle-class family just after the turn of the century and brought up by nannies and in boarding schools, Bowlby's later work with delinquent children, children in residential care and studies of animals, suggested that children who were separated from their mothers in the first five years could be psychologically damaged in a way that might undermine their adult lives; their 'insecure' attachments to their early carers could make them liable to poor self-image, a sense of themselves as unlovable which in turn would hinder their ability to form close and meaningful relationships and possibly lead to anti-social behaviour.

By contrast, argued Bowlby, children with secure attachments (and he specified that this should be with the mother figure) were more likely to have positive self-images, form better social rela-tionships and live more fulfilled lives. In his 1951 report on Maternal Care and Mental Health, he stated bluntly: 'Maternal care in infancy and early childhood is essential for mental health. This is a discovery comparable to that of the role of vitamins in physical health.'

Bowlby's work coinciding with the period in which women's employment was starting its rapid rise inevitably led to much hand-wringing about the effects of mothers who worked. By the time his report into maternal care and mental health was republished in 1965, society was on the cusp of a revolution for women. The end of the marriage bar in some professions, the arrival of the Pill and key landmarks in equal opportunities and sex discrimination legis-lation from 1971 onwards subsequently set Bowlby on a collision course with the burgeoning feminist movement.

In the intervening years, volumes of analysis and research have been devoted to picking over Bowlby's theory. Indeed, academics are still agonising over the evidence for and against Bowlby, analysing how effective his studies were and trying to evolve public policy, especially with regard to childcare, sensitively. Much of the later work contests Bowlby's research and the context in which many of the children he studied were brought up, often with much longer periods of separation from the mother – for reasons such as imprisonment, evacuation or illness – than a full-time job might require. This in itself may have meant other traumatic events influenced the long-term well-being of the children he studied. However, it sometimes seems as if the ghost of Bowlby, who died in 1990, is alive and well and haunting the ongoing debate about policies for working families. Only recently, senior Tory politician Iain Duncan Smith stated categorically that the rise in antisocial behaviour could be linked to women being 'pressurised' into going back to work soon after their children are born, suggesting that only maternal care twenty-four hours a day, seven days a week, can lead to good outcomes for children.

And while no one would dispute that the relationships both parents form with their children in the first year of life are crucial, there is little evidence to prove categorically that a good outcome rests solely with the mother. In fact it is now generally accepted that children can form secure attachments to other people in their early years, but it is the stability and quality of that care that is crucial. Children can flourish with a range of carers – a mix of grandparents, parents and a good childminder or nanny – as long as the routine remains stable and the main carers are loving, responsive and always aware of the baby's needs.

Child and adolescent psychiatrist Sebastian Kraemer, an honorary consultant at London's Tavistock Clinic, argues that the gravest misunderstanding to emerge from Bowlby's work was that infants had to be cared for only by their mothers.

'Women heard of Bowlby's work and believed that they were being told that unless they spent every minute of the day and night with their infants they would damage them forever,' he says. 'No doubt some mothers did not realise how much their children needed adult human company – it was quite common practice, for example, to leave babies in the pram outside to be "aired" most of the day. But of course it was a terrible misunderstanding, not helped by the prevailing custom and Bowlby's own limited social experience, to think that continuous care meant that only one person had to provide it ... attachment is often misunderstood as a kind of instant bond, like superglue, as if one needed to get stuck to the parent and hold on for ever. It really is the opposite, more like a flexible gravitational force.'

A more reassuring interpretation of the 'good enough mother' came from another prominent mid 20th-century child psychoanalyst, Donald Winnicott, who saw a more subtle development of the mother-baby relationship from the early months when the baby is utterly vulnerable and dependent, through to an inevitable and healthily managed separation as the baby learns to become more independent and to cope with his mother's gradual disengagement. 'The good enough mother ... starts off with an almost complete adaptation to her infant's needs and as time proceeds she adapts less and less completely, gradually, according to the infant's growing ability to deal with her failure,' he wrote.

Both mother and baby need time to adapt to that separation, which is why being able to afford to take longer maternity leave can make a huge difference to the process of going back to work. Future changes in maternity pay should reflect the lack of choice currently available for lone parents, or mothers without well-paid partners or occupational maternity pay to back them up.

Angela's return to work after four months felt too soon, though she did feel happier after the family found a nursery place and got rid of the nanny: 'I didn't have the sort of anxiety leaving her in the nursery that I felt leaving her at home with the nanny. She seemed so happy and she got on ever so well with all the staff and they loved her but I still felt that pull. I did my work and I know I did it well and managed a successful team of people under me, but I could never hang around at the end of the day. That pull, it never goes away'.

So in spite of her affection for her boss and the stimulation she got from her job in the pharmaceutical industry, she eventually handed in her notice. 'I knew I could never really go anywhere as a career in that job, or push my career forward and I really didn't want to. I was tired and there was always this feeling at the back of my mind that I had a child at home.'

Returning to work, maybe too early or simply for too many hours every day, can put relationships both at home and between mother and baby under too much strain. Learning how to 'read' your baby while you are on maternity leave should help you to distinguish between the sort of healthy manageable emotions that inevitably arise from separation and something more that is unmanageable either for the mother or the baby.

That 'tipping point' moment, when you realise that your domestic arrangements or your working arrangements aren't right, can come at any stage. Some mothers manage the initial return to work quite easily, only to find that later on, maybe with one or two more children, arrangements that may have seemed very successful in the first year, suddenly stop working, or that once their children hit the teenage years, work-life balance arrangements need to shift gear again.

Whenever the tipping point strikes, as Angela and many other mothers have found out, this can lead to having to arrange different working hours, patterns or even different jobs.

That decision triggered a series of changes in the family's life. They moved to a less expensive rural area which was closer to other family members. The move gave the couple financial freedom but, like many women who find the pull of motherhood temporarily stronger than the desire to pursue a full-time career, the thought of doing absolutely nothing quickly wore off and Angela adapted to her new situation by completing a part-time interior design course which eventually helped her to start her own business.

She became pregnant again shortly afterwards and managed to claw back the 'bonding' time she felt she had missed with her first daughter in the six months before the second baby arrived. 'That is a time I would never have given away. It was lovely, we'd sit on the sofa and just sort of cuddle and she'd say, "Mummy, I'll look after you." It was just such a special time and I still regret not having had more time like that with her when she was younger.'

Ironically, when her second daughter was born and the anxiety about separation was removed, Angela found herself adopting a much more matter-of-fact approach to motherhood. Knowing that she had ample time to bond with her second daughter she gave up breastfeeding earlier with complete confidence. 'It was just a sort of decision. I thought I have had enough of this, I wanted my body back and everything was gearing up with the business and all my coursework. I was more ambitious.'

The fact that Angela, the same mother, had two entirely different experiences with each daughter only proves how problematic it is either to prescribe a right or wrong way to manage separation and returning to work, or for legislators to frame the law in a way that allows each family to make the right choices for them.

Child and adolescent psychiatrist Sebastian Kraemer says that trying to agree the right fixed times for mothers to wean or to go back to work is impossible. 'Some children are babies for longer than others. I agree that's hard for policymakers who can't get to know every baby. But the calendar cut-off is not the most helpful measure.'

The optimum time may be linked to whether mothers are breast-feeding or not. Moving a baby to bottle-feeding or weaning on to solids can start that subtle process of separation but this time is also overlaid with physical and emotional reminders that the initial intimacy between mother and baby is coming to an end. The sensation of milk welling up inside her only heightened Dee's anxiety as she waited for a crowded, overheated Tube train to get to work. And even though Angela lived close enough to her office to be able to walk home at lunchtime, her attempts to continue breastfeeding after she went back to work weren't successful, although she did try to express and save milk for her daughter. 'I actually carried on for five months, but she kind of pushed me away at that point and when I went home it didn't always work.'

There are now stricter guidelines for employers than existed when Angela's first baby was born. Even though the legal obligation is only for employers to provide suitable rest facilities for pregnant women or breastfeeding mothers, it is considered good practice for employers to have a policy that supports new mothers who want to continue breastfeeding. This should include a break in a warm, clean room (definitely *not* the toilet) so mothers can express milk, and a fridge in which to store it. Women who want to express milk when back at work should write to their employers before returning so a risk assessment can be carried out.

That may sound fine on paper, but for women who attempt to manage a return to work armed with a breast pump, the reality is often complicated, embarrassing and at times comic, according to one mother who tried it twice. Ruth was a senior civil servant when her first son Jamie was born. She went back to work quickly, when he was eighteen weeks old, but only for two days a week to lead a departmental review. A tall, striking women, she is blunt about going back to work: 'I didn't find re-entry into the workplace that tricky, as I was only in the office two days a week and I was totally focused on the job when I was there.

'But I really enjoyed breastfeeding and I was also aware of the health benefits, especially as I have asthma and wanted to make sure both boys got as much of my milk as possible. There were five days of the week when I was able to feed Jamie throughout the day so I really didn't want the two days in the office to dictate what happened the rest of the week. But trying to manage the pump at work was a bit of a nightmare that required a healthy dose of self-deprecation and ability to laugh at oneself.'

Ruth started out with the idea that she would be able to express milk at work, and carefully take it home at the end of the day to feed to the baby.

'That didn't last long. It was just all too difficult, embarrassing and awkward. I wasn't organised enough, or pedantic enough, to have "breastfeeding slots" timetabled into my Outlook diary or anything like that.

'My plan, if there was one, was just to slip out to the loo at convenient moments to express. This meant that I'd continually find myself in the middle of critical meetings – often with very senior people – which ran well over schedule. I'd suddenly realise that my breasts felt like they were about to explode or, worse, were leaking milk everywhere and it was impossible to excuse myself. That was where a high level of personal composure plus the sense of humour were absolutely necessary. You couldn't duck out of the meeting as if you were just going to the loo, because you knew that expressing would take a good five to ten minutes, so you'd sit tight, desperately hoping the meeting was going to finish quickly and that no one else had noticed anything abnormal.'

In spite of the fact that she worked in a government department, the only place available to express was the ladies' toilet. 'I remember feeling a bit self-conscious about having to walk across the office with all the expressing paraphernalia in a plastic bag,' she recalls. 'Once I got to the loo it was OK – I'd just sit in a cubicle and get on with it. I was definitely extremely fortunate; I didn't find expressing difficult, and I could do it pretty speedily but I did feel embarrassed on occasions, mainly because it's not a silent activity, even with a hand-held pump. When someone else was using the cubicle next to me, I'd sit silently and wait for them to finish and leave before recommencing.

'Then once you have finished expressing, you have to deal with the product. At first I tried to keep the milk in the staff fridge, but I did feel that was a bit weird for other staff to come across. Even if you put things in a bag in the fridge, people would always rootle through other people's lunches, etc., looking for milk or butter or whatever so there was a high likelihood of it being found.

'I once managed to spill the contents of a bottle of expressed milk all over someone's carefully wrapped ham and cheese sandwiches. I panicked, tried to shake and wipe the milk off the clingfilm, and just put the sandwiches back in the fridge, hoping that the owner would assume it was cow's milk if they noticed.

'But to be honest, it quickly just became much easier for expressing to be all about getting rid of excess milk and nothing more. Trying to keep the milk and take it home was just far too ambitious, especially as it also meant sterilising everything at work before the second use.'

Now working from home as a consultant to the public sector, and with a second, longer maternity leave to reflect on, Ruth believes that the onus should be more on employers to actively support a new mother's wish to express milk and continue breastfeeding.

'It would be good if employers could enquire politely about expressing, show they understood the issues, and to encourage women to plan their expressing times into their diary and protect them. But you would need to be careful. Some women would not like to have that conversation with their manager – male or female.

'There's something funny about the business of expressing. It's a slightly strange, mechanical activity but also more personal than breastfeeding. I never felt in the slightest bit awkward about breastfeeding the boys, even in public. But somehow appearing with breast pump paraphernalia amongst work colleagues felt like drawing people's attention to something way too personal. Lots of people – men especially – who might be OK about breastfeeding wouldn't even know what expressing was, or why you might do it. So I suppose I did try to keep it quiet; I don't think any of my colleagues would have known I was expressing at work.'

And going back when her second son, Finlay, was seven months old made a big difference, on all sorts of levels, but particularly in terms of expressing milk at work.

'He'd already dropped a daytime feed or two by the time I went back, so I think I only needed to express once a day at work, and only for a few weeks. I continued happily breastfeeding morning and night until he was ten months old – the only problem was occasionally not getting home in time for his night-time feed.

'I was in a department which had many more women working in it, and our work focused a great deal on families, parents and the early years, so talking about expressing was much easier. Having said that, I don't think the department was particularly supportive – all the same practical issues remained. There was nowhere particularly suitable for expressing. Still the same old communal fridge problems were there but these issues were just less acute because Fin was that much older when I went back.'

The period between six and twelve months sees a rapid transformation in the baby's world, not just in their feeding habits. By six months they are becoming more aware of their bodies and also being more responsive and aware of other people in their inner circle beyond that all-encompassing relationship with their mothers. Separating our own anxieties from the baby's understandable response to a major change like its mother being absent for longer periods of time can be tricky, but babies and children are tougher than we think and, given the right foundations, will happily move on to the next stage in their development. It is arguably harder for us because of the adult guilt we inevitably feel which may be compounded by a too-early return or going back to a job that you may not particularly like or feel forced to do for financial reasons.

Sophie Boswell, a psychotherapist at London's Tavistock Clinic, has written in detail about how a parent's emotions and experiences are woven into those of their babies in the first year. Some guilt is inevitable during the journey back to work.

'Transitions such as these do involve loss and will never be achieved without some sadness, anger and anxiety on both sides. However, neither experience needs to be traumatic as long as it is handled sensitively. If the baby's parents are able to remain in touch with themselves and with their baby, letting her see that her feelings will be accepted and understood, she can learn that change and loss are painful, but manageable – and that they can yield new opportunities too,' she writes.

Managing our own guilt and helping babies cope depends not just on the work environment – going back to a job you love and are ready to restart makes a huge difference – but also on the amount of support mothers get from family, friends and colleagues at work.

And far from being damaging, introducing another carer who is well trained and loving may even be beneficial for the mother and baby. Sebastian Kraemer sees happy babies existing as part of a 'social system' that includes the baby, the mother, the wider family who support the parents and others who take an active part in caring. 'The relationship between mother and child is like a wedge which gets thinner and thinner as the intense need for the primary attachments lessens and the father, siblings, carers, grandparents come in until the young adult has Mum and Dad and a wide range of friends. At best, childcare is part of that story but that means that the minders and carers need a lot of training and ongoing support.'

An isolated mother with no help, no one to talk to and no prospect of returning to work may even be damaging as it can lead to post-natal depression. 'A baby can be with its mother and still be separated,' explains Sebastian Kraemer, 'especially if the mother is anxious or depressed or guilty. You should not be doing it on your own. A mother doing it on her own twenty-four hours a day is complete madness.'

Depression and isolation can also lead to a vicious circle in which returning to work becomes almost impossible. Now well established in a major UK university where she raises funds for academic research, Beverly, a petite and poised mother of two who worked as a scientist before the birth of her first child, found herself in a downward spiral when she gave up her job after the baby's birth.

At that time she and her husband were living in the USA, where the maternity leave was poor. 'As soon as I had her I realised I just couldn't go back – the plan was to put her in a nursery on the campus and go back to work but in the States the maternity leave is just shocking. I was offered three months, only six weeks of which was partially paid. I just wasn't ready to hand over my baby, to be honest. I realised pretty much right away that I didn't want to be apart from her.'

Even though Beverly's employers were willing to offer part-time work, her visa situation made this impossible. Quitting her job straight away meant she lost her work visa, which prevented her from applying for other part-time posts that would have allowed her to spend more time at home with her daughter. However, the isolation, the lack of any support from friends and family who were thousands of miles away in the UK, the exhaustion and the long absences while her husband was away took their toll.

'I was diagnosed with post-natal depression around five months after she was born. I didn't initially realise it, I just thought I was really tired because I had a new baby, I was breastfeeding and didn't have any support because my husband worked and travelled a lot so he was away most of the week, or all of the week in fact sometimes. I physically couldn't have gone back to work and I think the post-natal depression caused a lack of confidence overall in my life and in the end was the reason we came home.'

Good counselling and drug treatment helped her recover and she is now happily settled in the UK and has a new career as well as a second child. But the intense emotions of those early months are still vivid: 'When I had my daughter, I felt a bit lost. It was such a humungous shock to go from being very busy having the career, having a good social life, and travelling a lot, to just coming to a standstill. I was miles away from my family with very few friends who had children. I didn't really know anyone else with babies, I had always had my own money and been independent and then I had to go to having absolutely nothing.'

Is it possible to create a 'perfect storm' of circumstances that can allow the sort of healthy separation that plays a part in helping your baby develop into a resilient toddler while also protecting your own emotional well-being? The early months before you return to work form crucial building blocks in a responsive, intuitive relationship that needs to last a lifetime. Understanding how your relationship with your baby can secure those strong foundations may well come naturally. For many women it sounds like common sense to soothe a crying baby, or engage a baby who is restless, by rocking or lowering voice tone a level. But how we respond to our babies in those early months may be affected by a whole host of factors: exhaustion, some post-natal depression, the stress of managing older children, the pressure of a first baby on your relationship with your partner, how we were brought up ourselves and even our own relationships with our mothers.

Some women don't feel that they slip into motherhood easily, while others may want support and advice, but feel afraid or ashamed to ask for it. There is an increasing number of organisations that work with new parents, both mothers and fathers, to help them in those early months. Many of them concentrate as much on the emotional aspects of strengthening the mother-baby bond as on the practical aspects of being responsible for a new child, in particular encouraging parents to talk about their feelings about being a parent, to reflect on how their own parents related to them and to understand how to 'read' their baby and respond to the baby's signals whether they are hungry, hot, cold, distressed or happy.

One of these organisations – OXPIP, the Oxford Parent Infant Project – concentrates on helping parents and babies develop a more secure and loving relationship principally by encouraging parents to observe their babies closely, to notice their babies' behaviour and feelings and to help parents to think about their meaning. Co-founder and psychotherapist Sue Gerhardt, author of *Why Love Matters*, a book which explores how the early relationships between parents and their babies can affect children's later lives, sees the first year split into two distinct phases: 'The first six months are really important for establishing a sense of basic safety, an ability to regulate the body and its various states, which comes out of good regulation by a parent figure who is sensitive to the baby's needs. Future stress regulation may depend on these early experiences. The baby is also getting the hang of social interaction as a kind of dialogue where people respond to each other and affect each other.'

The second sixth months is likely to be the time in which your baby will need to get used to another carer and Gerhardt argues this time is maybe more important. 'In this period, the baby is building up an understanding of how the immediate social world responds to him or her – does the caregiver notice his needs and respond quickly and appropriately, or does the baby have to learn to suppress his needs to fit in with others, or exaggerate them to get a response?

'By about one year old, the baby has got a pretty good idea of what people close to him are like and what is the best way of responding to them. So the people he or she interacts with in this second part of the first year are very significant for his social development and set up expectations of how to get his needs met by others.

'At any point in this vital early period, what's important is that the people who look after the baby are sensitive, responsive and can read the baby's non-verbal signals. This is a lot easier if there is continuity of care from one or two people over the period. But if the baby is with the mother for the first six months, and then goes to another caregiver who is equally sensitive and responsive, all should be well – the baby can make a secondary attachment and still feel confident that other people will take good care of him, which is the main thing. The problem comes if the second caregiver isn't that sensitive or available, so it is crucial to make sure that you have confidence in the emotional capacities of the person you hand your baby over to; they will be helping to shape your baby's emotional regulation and understanding of how to relate to others.'

Many women do find the sensitive, responsive care that makes going back to work easier rather than a struggle. Although in the UK around half of all mothers are back at work within a year, around two-thirds of those don't go back until their babies are at least six months old and then mainly to part-time work. Finding the right carer can, after a positive, happy maternity-leave period in which you have bonded well with your baby, be the right spring-board for work, especially if to a challenging, stimulating job.

The signs of her young family are all over Emma's terraced house in Cambridge. At home with her second baby, still breast-feeding, she admits to loving the chance to be a full-time mum for a year before she goes back to work again. She radiates a sense of complete certainty that returning to work for the second time is the right thing for her to do.

When her first child was born she was doing a job in publishing that she loved and had been commuting for six years between London and Cambridge. Even though her employers were enlight-ened and offered generous flexible working arrangements, she decided she wanted to avoid the two-hour daily journey and while on maternity leave, she found a better job locally in the same field of scientific and medical publishing, where she would work only four days a week. So close to home was the new job that she could eventually put her young daughter on the back of her bike, cycle to the childminder and then into work, making the process almost painless. As her husband was able to pick the baby up later in the day, she didn't have to rush back in the evening. In her first year back at work she managed two substantial trips abroad with ease.

'I suppose it sounds awful but no, I didn't find it difficult. My daughter was on solids and I was very comfortable with the idea of going back to work. I wanted to start thinking in a different way and was worried that I might go rusty. The hardest thing for me was going into a new job rather than leaving her but I had extended my maternity leave twice from six months and eventually from nine months.'

Finding the right childcare to fit in with a job she actively wanted to do removed any lingering doubts that Emma and her husband may have had about her return to work. The couple chose a husband and wife child-minding team who were highly rated by Ofsted, the government inspectorate, because they liked the idea of continuity of care and having someone nearby whose home their daughter went to every day. Those extra months of maternity leave allowed a transitional period while Edie got used to going to the childminder before Emma started her new job and the family quickly slipped into the new routine.

A smooth return from maternity leave, a hands-on partner, family-friendly employer and an interesting job; it's the 'perfect storm' if you are lucky enough to be able to ensure all four mesh together. The one drawback of extending maternity leave can be that an otherwise easy baby who has grown used to a wider group of carers can appear to slip backwards as 'separation anxiety' starts at around seven or eight months, just at the point that women who are making use of the longer leave entitlement are going back to work. Emma admits that her daughter would sometimes be quite clingy, but separation anxiety is quite normal as babies start to learn more about their own feelings, developing the capacity to notice other people's feelings and also starting to understand how to manipulate and test the responses of those who care most about them.

Even so it can be unsettling to see a baby, who might have already appeared to be adapting well to another carer, suddenly become more anxious and clingy, crying inconsolably when you are about to leave or becoming hard to settle. That can put an extra burden on those first few months back at work, even though they do eventually pass through this phase – separation anxiety usually subsides by about fifteen or sixteen months. The invisible umbilical cord is never more present than when you are faced with walking out the door leaving a screaming infant behind. The child development expert Penelope Leach explains it from the baby's point of view: 'When the baby loses sight of you she minds. You are the centre of her world, the mirror in which she sees herself and everything else, and her manager who copes with her and helps her cope with other things. When you go away from her you know where you are going, but she does not. As far as she is concerned you might be gone forever. Out of sight is out of mind.'

Many mothers only find out about the upset that separation anxiety can trigger once it is too late and they have had a miserable few months back at work, feeling doubly guilty about leaving a baby who suddenly seems anxious and miserable in a way they weren't before. Amelia, formerly a primary school teacher who re-trained as an educational psychologist, found herself in an almost parallel situation to Emma when contemplating going back to a four-day week both with her first daughter, now four, and more recently her baby son.

Both children settled quickly with a local childminder, whose home was a ten-minute walk from the family's West London terraced cottage. However, Amelia made a conscious decision to bring her return to work forward after her first maternity leave, so she went back when her daughter was seven months old, specifi-cally to *avoid* the risk of separation anxiety. The confidence she had in that decision owed a lot to her own professional knowledge about child development.

'It was actually a colleague at work who first pointed out that going back to work before the separation anxiety set in was a good idea,' she explained. 'I found it helpful on several levels. It gave me a good reason to offer people who wanted to know why I wasn't taking my full entitlement, because there is a feeling around these days that you are letting your children down if you go back to work too soon.

'But actually I may have been doing her a favour. She started going to the childminder for one day a week before I went back, and when I did go back for four days a week, she barely seemed to notice. I am convinced that because she started bonding with the childminder a little bit earlier than she might have done if I had stayed off for longer, their relationship has been stronger than it would have been if I had left it a few more months. She even called her mummy sometimes, which I didn't mind at all because it gave me confidence that she was happy.

'And they have an incredibly close bond even now that she has started school. She will often wake up in the morning and start the day by asking what I think Lauren, the childminder, is doing today.'

You and your baby will survive if you have formed that secure relationship, coped with earlier separations, and the baby is used to the carer. Even though she didn't go back to work until her daughter was nine months old, Emma found her childminder several months before and spent time getting her daughter used to the new environment. Leach says that surviving the separation anxiety depends on the baby having another special person whom she can use as her 'completing half' and with whom she has a strong loving relationship until you come back: 'Leave your baby with such a person and even if you leave her apparently drowning in a sea of despair, she will be safely aboard the life raft of that relationship within minutes of your departure.'

Babies may be perfectly happy with their childminders or at nursery but that doesn't mean they aren't missing their mothers and sometimes they will only display those tumultuous emotions when you return. However tired and stressed you are – and my most hated moment of the day as a working mother was that walk through the door at the end of the evening when you have to snap instantly back into mum mode when your body is screaming to just sit down and unwind with a glass of wine – it is always best to try and perfect a cheery loving departure and a positive happy return so that the baby knows that when you do go away, you do come back and are happy to see him or her. It may be tempting to slip away and hope your baby won't notice. We have all done it, but that might only make the situation worse.

There will inevitably be a sense of loss on both sides, just as there is when you stop breastfeeding, say goodbye that first time at the school gate, realise your easy-going child has turned into an alien and recalcitrant teenager and the same feeling can even take you by surprise when you bid them farewell as they depart for university. The pain of being separated from a much-loved child can strike at any time. After my own agonising journey back to work when my elder son was twelve weeks old, which eventually led to me resigning my then job, I then went to the other extreme and worked from home when the second two were tiny, but eighteen years later found the departure of our second son, and his subsequent homesickness, heart-wrenching. He is fine now but clearly we had to have our separation moment at some point.

As Rozsika Parker, in her book *Torn in Two*, writes: 'Mother and child face the task of negotiating a sequence of separations from the moment of birth onwards. However, while children move with more or less difficulty towards an ever-increasing sense of themselves as individuals separate from their mothers, women evolve from one maternal identity to another. Thus they move from being a mother supporting a head, to a mother pushing a buggy, to a mother holding a hand, to a mother waving a hand, to a mother waiting for a hand to hold. *But always a mother.* Theirs is a vertical development compared to their children's more "horizontal" growth away from them.'

CHAPTER 2

The Juggling Act

Going back to work doesn't need to be a process fraught with anxiety and guilt. Many women manage it relatively painlessly and then sustain careers, get promoted and adapt their jobs to fit their new roles as mothers. It's rarely effortless, but it can be done. Over coffee in the busy health club close to her office in the Surrey stockbroker belt, which she uses regularly as a break from her job as a senior sales executive, Caitlin, a tall, energetic forty-year-old, can chart an almost seamless succession of jobs since the birth of her first daughter when she was twenty-nine.

Caitlin took six months off after the birth of each of her two girls, Amy and Kate, and while she admits that she went back to work just as her children were, from her point of view, starting to get more interesting, she had no doubt that it was the right thing to do.

'I always knew I wanted to get into a job in the commercial sector and I knew I wanted to have an interesting job,' she explains. Her decision was also guided by the fact that her husband's family had a history of depressive and stress-related mental illness. 'One of the things he always said to me was that he never ever wanted to be the only wage earner because he felt that would put tremendous pressure and stress on him.'

Both graduates and exactly the same age, Caitlin and Tim struck a deal over work and family that has lasted more than twelve years. During that time Caitlin has moved jobs, cajoled and confronted various employers to ensure that her working hours matched her family's needs while maintaining status and her level of pay. This is no mean feat in an age where two-thirds of working-age women with dependent children are in work but are often doing jobs for which they are over-educated or too skilled. Many women are in such jobs because they allow more flexibility, or simply because chopping and changing employers to fit in with family responsibilities leads to a loss in work experience, bargaining power and, over time, status and income.

Some women do give up working completely once they have children, with an intention to go back at some stage in the future, an aspiration that is often hard to fulfil. But most women who were working full-time before they got pregnant do go back to work in the first year, often initially to the jobs they did before they got pregnant. That, however, does not always last: one recent study suggested that a year after the first birth only 40 per cent of women are still in full-time employment and that the movement from full-time to part-time work appears irreversible. Only 58 per cent of working women who no longer have dependent children are in full-time work compared to 96 per cent of their male counterparts.

Another study which followed the work choices of four hundred first-time mothers suggested that of the 80 per cent who had planned to return to work, just over a half were part-time and the rest full-time. However, after the baby's birth only around three-quarters were working in the way they had intended, with 10 per cent of the full-timers going part-time and 14 per cent not working at all. The women were questioned again when their children were three and only just over 1 per cent said they would want both partners to be working full-time. The reasons women had given for not returning to work in the way they had planned were stress and exhaustion, the cost of childcare, a child's illness, a strong emotional urge to be with their child or an intransigent employer.

There is no doubt that for most women, the relationship with their employer changes after maternity leave. Having agreed with her husband that she would go back to work, Caitlin successfully managed her full-time job in a large multi-national company when her first daughter was a baby but was the first person ever to ask to work a four-day week in the company where she was a senior sales manager, when her second daughter was born. 'It is quite interesting looking back on what it was like when I started there. Nobody wore trousers to work, we all wore skirts and even though change started to come slowly and we were eventually allowed to start wearing trousers there were still certain sales directors who expected you to wear a jacket if you went to see them. So that gives you a picture of how old-fashioned it was in many ways. All the sales controllers were men, all the national account managers were men and the only women were among the secretaries or support staff.

'I was one of the first women to become a national account manager and even though there were good maternity entitlements, because it was a very big international company, there still weren't many women at that level who had had babies before. I was probably the first one to have gone on maternity leave and then asked, and been allowed, to work part-time.

'Even so, that coincided with a regrading of all the jobs and when I was given the regrading for my job it was a grade lower than the job I had been doing before. It wasn't less money but it was lower in terms of status and I would have had to get a promotion to get back up to where I was.

'I just said to them, "Look, I could take you to a tribunal for doing this because this is a job that isn't of equal status to the one I've left." Anyway that was enough for them to think they ought to regrade the job so I didn't lose any status; they paid me pro rata, four days a week, twenty days' holiday and I even told them they should have pro-rata'd my car and they let me keep the same car that I was entitled to as a full-time worker.

'But it was a big company and they could afford to do things like that and I have to say the floodgates then opened and everyone who thought they might be able to do it asked to. When another girl, who just got pregnant after me, went on a maternity leave a year later, they let her come back part-time as a national account manager so that's how things had moved in a year. They changed massively.'

Many employers, especially big private sector companies and the public sector (now under a new legal requirement to promote more equality between male and female employees), are slowly changing their approach to working mothers in the light of changes in the law relating to maternity pay, leave and flexible working. Some now offer exemplary return-to-work schemes with imaginative flexible working arrangements, conscious that this will help them to retain women workers and attract younger graduates who increasingly list work-life balance as a priority when they are looking for jobs.

However when *The Apprentice* television show presenter Sir Alan Sugar recently claimed that many bosses now immediately bin job applications from women of child-bearing age he gave voice to the deeply held assumptions that still exist among many employers about working mothers and which are felt on a daily basis by the women who work for them.

Several of the more conservative employers' organisations have echoed his prejudices. The Institute of Directors, for example, regularly questions the need to enshrine flexible working in legislation. Media commentator and former Institute of Directors policy director Ruth Lea has described the allegation that employees, and particularly women with children, find it difficult to achieve a balance between home and work as 'partly urban myth and partly a sentimentalised retreat from reality'. Campaigners for more flexible working arrangements were described by her as 'polemicists and lobbyists' who were effectively 'demonising the workplace'.

Most new mothers are entitled to return to the jobs they had before they were pregnant. If, for some reason, their employers can't offer them the same job, or the post has been made redundant, they *should* be offered suitable alternative work. If the job has changed in any other way, they should be entitled to terms and conditions that are as favourable as those enjoyed before taking maternity leave.

Employers are now encouraged to offer 'Keeping in Touch' days which allow women on maternity leave to work up to ten days within that period, apart from the compulsory two-week maternity leave period immediately after the birth. In theory, anyone given a different job on their return to work as a result of their maternity leave could make a discrimination claim, although in practice these are hard to sustain.

Women who stick with the jobs they did before they left on maternity leave tend to suffer less from occupational downgrading, even if they do successfully negotiate more flexible working arrangements and, like Caitlin, start to change the culture in their own workplaces.

Now living in a sparsely furnished terraced house in north Manchester, Nancy, a slim, blonde single mum in her late thirties, recognises that her decision to return to her job in local government, after she gave birth to her only child, eight-year-old Iona, proved to be her lifeline when her marriage subsequently broke up.

'I couldn't wait to get back to work,' she explains. 'I thought I would be a real earth mother but none of my friends had babies then, so there was just nothing to do and it was just boring. My employers were very understanding. I found a nursery for my daughter and she settled in really well. I originally intended to go back only four days a week but then my boss told me she was taking early retirement and to try out for the job. I went back in the January and I became the manager in the July and pulled out of going part-time.'

When her marriage disintegrated two years later, the job gave her an ability to support her daughter – and her own self-esteem. The circumstances were traumatic and acrimonious as she discovered her husband hadn't paid the mortgage for eight months while her salary had been covering all the remaining family costs.

'It was the most awful time in my life. I had to sell the house, and borrow money from a friend and move here. I couldn't get on the housing list because I worked full-time and I wasn't on benefits. I couldn't even think about giving up my job because I felt I would have had no security. I wasn't brought up to live on benefits. My mother always worked and made us all work to earn money. She always had part-time jobs even when she was older. It never crossed my mind not to work.

'My head was in pieces and I probably should have got some professional help but I knew I had to keep the job going for my daughter's sake.'

The strength of the relationship with her employers helped her to negotiate a system of flexible working based on 'compressed hours', which now allows her to start early on some days and leave at 3pm twice a week. She also stores hours to free up time in the school holidays when Iona isn't staying with her parents, who live an hour away from Nancy's home.

'I think if it was starting to affect Iona then I would change, but at the moment I do devote all my time to her and to my job but I think it would frighten me to go part-time because of the lack of money – I wouldn't survive.'

Nancy's system of compressed hours is tough. Her daughter is at school some distance from their new home, partly because Nancy had to find a school with after-school and breakfast club facilities. Mother and daughter frequently leave the house well before eight so Iona can have breakfast at school before Nancy heads off to work. Iona's mild special needs have meant mother and daughter often spend their evenings together going over school work. There is not much spare cash to spend at weekends and not much time to contemplate taking on a more demanding job or achieving more qualifications or training.

'My sister, who is very academic, is always telling me to do a university course but I haven't got the time or the energy. I could transfer to another job with the management skills that I have but I don't think I would be ready to start afresh. I just need to keep everything going for Iona. I am quite happy and proud of how far I have come because I could have just lived off benefits, but that wasn't the way I was brought up and I would have felt that I had failed.'

That sense of 'just keeping everything going' will resonate with countless working mothers. Without the overwhelming financial incentives like those that drive Nancy to stay in full-time work, the appeal of more flexible working arrangements or a part-time job seem alluring.

It isn't just the desire to be at home with the baby or small children that contributes to the sense of conflict, because few women now go straight from the slower, dreamy pace of what childbirth guru Sheila Kitzinger calls 'the baby moon' to the cut-and-thrust of working life. Most have a stopping-off point between the two, during which they gather new friendships and become part of different networks that grow and develop alongside the baby. So going back to work doesn't simply mean leaving home behind, with all the anxiety that entails: it means leaving behind an alternative, often supportive, social group, quite distinct from the professional friends or colleagues, made up of local mums and built around drop-in centres and playgrounds rather than the office canteen or pub.

Even though it can be a relief to have time out from conversations that can at times become claustrophobically mummy-orientated, being part of that local community is still a comfort zone which can seem deeply, and deceptively, seductive.

Especially so if you are trying to sustain relationships with other local mothers while re-engaging work or if you find yourself in a hostile working environment. The temptation to take any alternative job offered, if that allows a bit more balance and time at home, or to drift out of work completely, can become overwhelming.

Seventeen years after she gave up her job in television when she was pregnant with her first child, Louise, a vivacious mother of two, still finds herself torn about the opportunities she missed, which now seem unattainable to her in her early forties.

Currently temping in London to bring in some extra money and give herself time at home with her two teenagers, Louise admits that at first she didn't try very hard to get back into work, mainly because she wanted to be at home with the children in the early years. But it became a habit she found hard to break, especially as she could never face handing them over to another carer: 'I don't like having other people in my house when I am not there, I don't even like the cleaners.'

An attempt to set up her own garden design business when the children were at primary school was only partially successful because the pull to be at home always trumped the job.

'I felt that someone would suffer if I went back full-time, either me or the kids. But now I realise that even if you don't work you suffer because you don't feel fulfilled. Being a parent is the best thing I have ever done – I haven't had as much fun as when I am at home with the children, but I have never cracked the work thing really and I do resent that. My biggest regret is not trying in some way to get back into BBC or television. I am an intelligent person and very organised. I should be in production management in television, and that would have been my goal if I had carried on.

'We were brought up to work and we were told to get out there and do it on our terms, but when I had the children I realised that I didn't think that was really achievable.'

The economist Catherine Hakim incurred the wrath of feminist colleagues when she suggested that the availability of contraception, the expansion of white-collar jobs which can be adapted to meet the needs of women who want to work part-time and the advent of equal opportunities policies meant that women may actually have *more* choices than men.

Her analysis of the female workforce divides women into 'home centred' types who prefer not to work, 'work centred' types who work full-time and the 'adaptive' type who juggles work and family and who she describes as the 'modern version of the homemaker', someone who fits work around the domestic role, often working part-time with breaks in employment, undoubtedly the most common choice made by most adult women with dependent children. 'In practice there is only one choice of work history for men, compared to three for women,' she wrote. 'Feminists who emphasise that women's choices are constrained and not completely free overlook the fact that women have more choices than men, who have none at all.'

The truth is almost certainly more complicated; many women, like Louise, try to balance their competing urges to be professionally successful and also to be good parents. Making a conscious decision to cut back work, go part-time, join the 'mummy track', whatever we choose to call it, usually follows a realisation that 'having it all' is a bit of a myth and that far from being liberated, working mothers are usually tied to what seem like two or three jobs in and out of the home.

But that choice often comes with strings attached. One study using the data from the British Household Panel Survey, a huge long-running survey of five thousand families, looked at how motherhood generally affects women's career prospects, and confirmed that the majority of new mothers who remain in work don't just switch to part-time employment but do 'trade down' as a result. Women in management positions are particularly badly affected and, although teaching and nursing are relatively good examples of professions that allow for part-time work in the same career, even in these professions one in ten women downgrade.

Almost half of all women professionals who do join what is often described as the 'mummy track' move into jobs where the average employee needs A levels rather than higher education, leaving thousands of women with families but also degrees, training or professional qualifications, completely underused.

Authors of the study, Dr Sara Connolly and Dr Mary Gregory, painted a bleak picture in their summary: 'From corporate manager to office worker. From teacher to classroom assistant, from nurse to care assistant. These are the occupational trajectories for some of Britain's most highly qualified women when they switch to part-time work and childcare. The loss of career status with part-time work is a stark failure among otherwise encouraging trends for women's advancement.

'Girls and young women are outperforming males at all educational levels. They are moving into an expanding range of occupations and building successful careers. The gender pay gap is narrowing but for many all this comes to an abrupt halt when childcare claims part of the working week.' The new Equalities and Human Rights Commission calls this haemorrhaging of women into lower-status, part-time work the 'hidden brain drain'.

But changes in status and job description might not always be a conscious choice. It is not unusual for women to return to work after maternity leave, possibly working reduced hours, and find a subtle, ingenious reworking of roles and responsibilities. Sangita was a high achiever in every sense of the word before she became pregnant. Active in local politics in the West Midlands and with a successful career in the voluntary sector, she was still determined to push ahead with her career and even managed to find a new job, managing a large team in a national charity, when her lively two-year-old, Manish, was only five weeks old. He was enrolled in a local authority nursery by the time he was four months and she started the job earlier than she had to, working three days a week initially with the intention that she would build up her hours and be back full-time by the time he was one.

'By that time my boss had made some changes in my responsibilities that I wasn't particularly happy with,' she explains. 'So I traded that for a four-day week. It took a significant chunk of work out of my domain and I did feel it was down to office politics, but if I had made a big play about it, I would have had to come back five days a week. I did think about fighting it, but you worry about what that looks like, it is a very small world and everyone knows each other and I just thought it is not badly paid, it is not a bad job and I can absorb the indignity of having a bit of work taken away from me.

'The compensating factor is really that I have managed to keep a four-day week and I get one day when I can do all the boring stuff like going to the doctor and cooking vast quantities of food to put in the freezer for the rest of the week and all of those mummy things that you have to do to keep family life ticking over.

Manish and I also get the chance to do something fun together, like having an afternoon out and it is just me and him and that is lovely.'

The trade-off between motherhood and job is one so many women will recognise and Sangita's case is proof that it is possible to trade down without it being catastrophic in career terms – even if she and her lawyer husband do feel they are permanently living 'one step away from chaos', as she cheerfully puts it. Her involvement in local politics – she is a local councillor – has helped to offset any sense that she may have sold herself short by giving up some of her management responsibilities and she has started planning her future, working out how she can repair the 'damage' that she feels has been done to her promotion chances. She is already looking for a new job that will help her to build them up again as her son gets older.

'I feel like life hangs together but if anything goes wrong it is a nightmare, like if one of us, or our son, is ill. If all three of us are ill then it is madness, anything that happens that throws you slightly off kilter is scary. Like when the nursery called to say a pylon had blown down and they were out of electricity for a week so they had to close. You just think how can this be happening to me.'

The new right to ask for flexible working hours may prove to be the middle way between giving up a hard-won career after maternity leave and drifting into a succession of less-challenging jobs. If politicians don't lose their nerve in more straitened economic times (and under pressure from employers' organisations) we should gradually reach a situation in which women can go back to the same job they had before they got pregnant, on their terms, maintaining confidence in themselves and the valuable work experience they need to move on to the next stage, when and if that feels right.

At the moment every employee who has been in a job for twenty-six weeks, with a child under six or caring for a disabled child under eighteen, can ask to work flexibly. Plans are under way to extend that right to all parents of children up to sixteen. Almost a half of new mothers now work flexitime compared to just 17 per cent in 2002 and a third of new dads too – almost three times as many as in 2002.

However, the jury is still out on the extent to which this will help mothers across the board. Some reports suggest that between 75 per cent and 90 per cent of requests to work flexibly are being agreed to. But an online survey of more than three thousand parents by the parenting websites Mumsnet and Dad.Info suggested that two-thirds of parents have still not been able to achieve the working arrangements they want and that a significant minority of men *and* women are being refused their requests to work flexibly and still worry about the long-term impact it would have on their promotion chances.

The charity Working Families campaigns for, and offers advice to, working parents. Calls to its helpline mostly come from pregnant women or new mothers concerned with their rights, or who feel they are being mistreated at work. This can mean anything from bullying and harassment to being refused the right to apply for flexible work and not getting either money or time off they are owed, says chief executive Sarah Jackson. She sees a polarisation between small- and medium-sized employers in non-urban areas and the bigger city firms. Many employees still don't feel they have the courage or energy to fight back when they are treated unfairly, she claims.

'Many of these bigger employers take their graduate recruitment very seriously and see the business case for more family-friendly working. The legislation that is in place is merely a foundation for them. Even though the early evidence suggests that most requests are successful, those figures hide a lot of requests that aren't successful. A lot of people who call our helpline tend to be working in low-income jobs and don't bother to ask because they won't get, so they can't see the point of trying. There is also a hidden statistic within that, which is that men are just as likely to be turned down as women, but fewer men ask. Masses of men would like to work flexibly but there is a whole pride thing: it can be very hard for a man to ask to work flexibly because it calls into question his masculinity and his role. We get a lot of calls from men who are getting bullied at work because they have asked for flexible hours, so there are still a lot of deep cultural issues that men too are fighting against.

'At worst this is about a loss of income and for women on a low income that can plunge them into poverty. But mostly it is about stress and distress because even if they are not losing their jobs, women are still being badly treated, they don't feel they have got the power to fight back; they won't try and take their employer to a tribunal because they fear they might lose their job.'

Disappointing as it may be to accept that the protection offered by the law is robust in theory but hard to enforce in practice, that is often the harsh reality. Anxiety about future job prospects in hard economic times may make women less willing to challenge discriminatory practices. Working Families is already reporting an increase in calls to its helpline from women facing redundancy or changes to their working arrangements, some of which, according to chief executive, Sarah Jackson, are blatantly discriminatory: 'A lot of employers are using the correct procedures but some are using the excuse of an economic downturn to get rid of women who are pregnant. So there might be one redundancy and it goes to the woman who is about to start her maternity leave. Another scenario we have seen is the woman who, having negotiated a part-time deal, is called ten days before she is due to go back to work and told she must come back full time. That woman is faced with a difficult choice – to challenge that decision or risk losing her job at a time of recession.' Going to a tribunal on any work-related issue at any time is complicated, expensive and not without the reputational risk that Sangita spotted when her new employer craftily redrafted her job description while she was working her way in after her maternity leave.

Employment lawyer Professor Aileen McColgan sees a slow cultural change amongst employers in the wake of the more recent employment and pro-working family legislation but also cautions strongly against legal action. 'Many employers now fear sex discrimination claims and the evidence suggests that many middle-class women assume they will take the full maternity leave; that is a change from ten to fifteen years ago. Also, innovations like the Keeping in Touch days are reducing the attrition rate with maternity.'

However, she still believes it is quite usual for women to have problems when they go back to work after childbirth. 'A woman may ask to change her job and a good employer will endeavour to accommodate her. Bad employers can't and won't. Likewise when employers try to change the woman's job on return they are usually slightly different in so many 'non-specific' ways. If women try to litigate on this, it is usually very difficult to pin down quite how they are different and the chances are that you will not be in that job in a year's time.

'Most workplace law needs to be enforced through tribunals. I would be dragged backwards over hot coals rather than do that. You can't win without expensive lawyers. Women can incur huge costs by suing employers while also alienating them. Even if you don't want to stay in the job and sue for constructive dismissal or victimisation, it could damage your prospects for other jobs. The best advice any woman can have is to join a union. Women need trade-union representation. The legal route is not a sensible one.'

She sees a particular problem for women in higher-status jobs like the law. 'Partners in city law firms probably can't negotiate down from the long hours for example, leaving at 7.30 or 8 at night because their clients expect them to be available all the time. Often they become support lawyers, still well paid but there is a loss of status. And there is still too much loss of women's talents when they downscale and do jobs they are overqualified for.'

A long drawn-out legal process is often unappealing if you are in two minds anyway about returning to work and there is money on the table for you to go. Like many older mothers who are well established in careers, Eve never thought she would be a 'stay at home mum' in the months leading to the birth of her first son when she was forty. She was a senior acquisitions editor in a large London publishing company with employers who were extremely sympathetic to her during her pregnancy, offering a range of flexible working conditions on return. However, while she was off on maternity leave the company made significant redundancies and required people to relocate outside London.

Now in a period out of work and mostly at home in the large

semi in the London suburbs that she shares with her husband Tom and two energetic little boys, she says the news came as a complete shock. 'I was thinking about arranging childcare because I wanted to come back to work. I never thought I would give up completely; all my friends who had had kids had gone back to work so my role models were all working mothers, and they *all* went back full-time.

'But that may have been naive. So many of the women I knew had their children a lot younger than me so by the time I got pregnant, their kids had grown up, and I wasn't really seeing them in the context I was in.

'I was on maternity leave when all the office closure stuff happened. There were lots and lots of rumours flying about so when Joe was about two months old I went in to discuss my future options, thinking I was going to have six months off, then suddenly it all changed. They shut the office and didn't give me much of a choice other than to tell me my job was redundant and that this was the package.

'I wasn't really even offered a job in the new office. I didn't think of challenging it and in a way I felt relieved, I mean I had money and time with my baby.'

In theory, anyone given a different job on their return to work or made redundant as a result of their maternity leave could make a legal challenge, although in practice these can be hard to win both legally and in personal terms. Eve would have had to prove that it wasn't a genuine redundancy and that someone else was doing her job and also prove that she was selected for redundancy because she had been pregnant and off on maternity leave: this could lead to a successful claim of unfair dismissal and sex discrimination.

Employers should prioritise finding an alternative job for women returning from maternity leave, a right which ceases once they return to work, but this might not always be a solution. What if Eve had been offered another job but in an office miles away? The job could have been the same but the journey may have made it impractical with small children at home. Taking the money can be the much easier path.

In Bridget's case, there wasn't even any financial compensation on offer. Challenging what she perceived to be a grossly unfair and discriminatory decision by her then employers to end her rolling contract after her second baby was born, proved bittersweet. She had her day in court, but ultimately failed to prove her claim of sex discrimination in a case that embodied all the difficulties and potential stress in pursuing employment claims.

A small feisty Scot, Bridget moved back north of the border after a twenty-year successful career in journalism in London. She negotiated a part-time contract with a national newspaper company which was renewed on an annual basis without any problems. Life with her photographer partner Alastair, in their spacious detached house in the countryside outside Glasgow, seemed idyllic until her first pregnancy ended in tragedy when she gave birth to a stillborn baby. Her employers were sympathetic and supportive; she went back to work soon after and was able to overcome her grief partly by submerging herself in the job. She had, therefore, no reason to suspect that there would be any difficulties when she got pregnant again two years later. By then in her mid-forties, she assumed that her contract would be renewed after the birth of her second child.

However, seven months into the pregnancy and before she had even had time to discuss how she would manage her maternity leave, her employers dropped their bombshell and informed her that the contract that had been rolled over for the previous seven years would not be renewed on the grounds that the company had to make rapid cuts in a financially difficult period (it subsequently transpired that other people would continue covering her work).

Advised by her partner not to spend the final few months of her pregnancy worrying about it, she concentrated on the birth of a healthy baby boy although the initial opinion of her trade union, that she may have a claim for sex discrimination, was still at the back of her mind and, when Calum was three months old, she decided she would take the case to a tribunal.

One of the factors in her decision was her age. 'I know we didn't need the stress but I also felt I had nothing to prove any more. I was forty-four, I had until then had a very good career, I had worked on national newspapers, travelled the world, there wasn't that much more I felt I needed to fulfil. Above all, I felt that I had been unfairly treated and I just thought unless someone stands up and says this is wrong, it will happen to other people, in particular women who might need the money much more than me.'

The case, supported by her union, finally reached the tribunal when her son was six months old and sitting in the car outside the court waiting to be breastfed. Direct sex discrimination is defined as occurring if an employer treats a woman less favourably than he or she would treat a man. Less favourable treatment on the ground of pregnancy is considered discriminatory but in Bridget's case the tribunal decided that she was unable to prove her case adequately and accepted her employer's assertion that her pregnancy hadn't played a part in their decision.

Providing that 'burden of proof' is notoriously difficult;

however, her disappointment at losing was tempered by the knowledge that she 'got her day in court' to make a public stand against what she perceived as blatant chauvinistic treatment. 'It was worth it just to know that all those executives were dragged up from London and had to sit there and be confronted with what they had done. I didn't need the money, I didn't feel I needed to protect my name but I can understand how difficult it would have been to pluck up the courage to do that if I had been younger and at the start of my career. Not many women have a baby at forty-four though, so professionally I was in a different situation and above all I had a healthy, much-wanted baby which was to me the most important thing.

'However, I also had a union to back me and too many women don't realise how important that is. My advice to every woman I know, whether they are friends or the checkout girls in the super-market – with whom I often get chatting about their kids and their jobs – is to join a union because you never know when you might need it.'

High-profile sex discrimination cases, such as the one brought by Andrea Madarassy, an equities banker who was made redundant while on maternity leave by Nomura International, only serve as reminders of how fiendishly complicated the law is, and how slim the chances of success are. Ms Madarassy was claiming £1 million compensation but lost because even though she may have been able to prove that she had been treated differently from other employees, the judge found that she couldn't prove that her treatment was a result of sex discrimination.

In another case, sales dealer Katharina Tofeji failed to convince a tribunal that she was a victim of sex discrimination, constructive dismissal and victimisation, dismissing claims that her former employers BNP Paribas refused to allow her flexible working after a year's maternity leave and refused to return the client list that she had successfully built up over the previous five years.

The tribunal didn't only throw out her claim for £1.35 million compensation, but the ensuing coverage of the case ensured that her relationship with her partner, her subsequent depression and claims that she was asked to use her sexuality to 'woo clients' were all aired publicly. During the case she alleged that one colleague had taken a bet on how long she would survive after she came back from leave and subsequently admitted that even if she were successful on appeal, her career in banking would be over.

The cases that hit the headlines are only the tip of an iceberg. A two-year investigation by the Equal Opportunities Commission into pregnancy discrimination found that almost half of the women surveyed had suffered some form of discrimination or unfavourable treatment while pregnant or on maternity leave.

Many were woefully ill-informed about their rights and often reported that pregnancy-related discrimination usually came down to relationships with individual managers or colleagues rather than institutional bias. Covert or overt antipathy from employers and colleagues, more subtle changes in working conditions, sexist bullying and underhand comments are even more difficult to challenge, yet can have an equally profound effect on individual women's longer-term attitudes to work, either making them more reluctant to return to work, stay with the same employers or to fight for their rights.

Now running her own successful public relations business, Jane can talk at length about what it feels like to be the victim of sly, insinuating discrimination. She is tall, striking and exudes confidence and it is hard to imagine her being intimidated by anyone. But as she acknowledges, in her large detached home on the outskirts of Leicester, pregnancy made her vulnerable in ways she would not have previously imagined possible during her ascent to becoming deputy news editor on a large regional daily paper.

So confident was she in her ability to do the job that she failed to see the warning signs when, in the early stages of pregnancy, she made a mistake in a story concerning a prominent local politician. She admits now that she was 'knackered all the time', working twelve-hour days. When her bosses called her in and suggested she might like to move to a different department for a 'quieter life' writing features, she confesses that she felt so 'pathetically grateful' that when they casually mentioned she would be taking a cut in pay, she acceded willingly.

'I just didn't have my head screwed on at the time. I know they couldn't get away with it now and they probably couldn't then and it is ridiculous that I didn't fight back. I was just really happy going in at nine, leaving at five and going to get my McDonald's thick shakes at lunchtime with no stress at all.'

Her employers also slipped in that she *shouldn't* consider coming back to work part-time to her original job, so after six months' maternity leave with less-than-generous occupational pay she was still 'just really grateful to have a job' and went back to the lower-status, lower-paid work three days a week out of fear that if she didn't, she would lose her job completely.

Over the next three years and the birth of another child, Jane admits to just 'hanging on'. Even though she hated leaving her children, she was too ashamed to admit to needing time off when they were ill and used to pretend she was sick instead. She persevered, convinced that she achieved more in her three days than many of her exclusively male colleagues did in a full week and was just keeping a lid on her anger: 'I felt all of that guilt of the part-time mum, I didn't go to the pub, I didn't go to lunch, I was highly organised. I'd have my interviews on one particular day, I'd take work home, and write things up there.'

Throughout it all, Jane experienced what she describes as systematic low-level bullying by some of her managers. 'There was an awful time where I was sitting at work one day and just rattling out something and one of the editors came round with an assistant and a clipboard. Gradually I realised that they were discussing moving my desk. When I asked what was going on, they replied, "You're only here three days a week and that's a bit of a waste of a desk so we're going to move you down to the copy takers' department".'

Jane remembers her sense of outrage: 'I just thought, this is my department, how dare you talk about me as a waste of a desk when I have worked my socks off and done over and over again what I was supposed to do. He was the same person who, when I went off on my maternity leave with my second child, came over to me and asked me if I was coming back and then laughed at me when I said I was. It was also quite common for colleagues to phone me at home to ask if I was coming back because they would "quite like my job".'

In the end Jane quit the job in favour of a job in PR that eventually led to her starting her own company. She became a round peg in a square hole, the working mum in an all-male, sexist environment who, though she had previously fitted in with the blokish culture – working long hours, going to the pub at the end of the day – suddenly found she was no longer a member. One of her lowest, and most humiliating, points came when she describes how she was made to feel when she was ordered into the office to write the front-page story on her day off, but had no childcare arranged so had to bring her baby to work with her. She was then accused by a colleague of being a hypocrite because in her pre-baby persona she used to take a dim view of anyone who brought their children into work.

In one of my stints as part-timer on a national daily paper, I remember working out that in the three days I worked I almost put in as many hours as the full-time male colleague who sat opposite me but used to arrive later, leave for the pub around midday, stay there for three hours, come back to the office for another two, before disappearing to the pub again at around the time I would leave for home. In a masterful display of male know-how, he would always position his jacket very visibly on the back of his chair so it would look as if he was temporarily away from his desk. No one questioned it. It was around that time that the Labour MP Harriet Harman coined the phrase 'presentism' to describe the phenomenon of men who were perceived to be at work simply because their coat was hanging on the back of the office door.

The sort of devious and crafty sexist attitudes that drove Jane out aren't only the preserve of male managers. Female colleagues can be as bad, if not worse, often specialising in a form of disapproval and resentment that is more nuanced and unspoken.

Anne, a secondary school teacher, describes the challenge of managing her largely female colleagues as 'much worse than any separation anxiety' when she went back as a part-time head of department after the birth of the first of her three daughters. Giving up work was never an option because the family needed two incomes to cover their mortgage. By the time she went back to work at the local community college in Surrey when her first daughter was eight months old, she had negotiated a four-day week, and a promotion which formed part of a job-share with another colleague. In every other sense her return to work was smooth. She and her husband David had full-time childcare from David's parents, who lived in a neighbouring village and had 'double sets of everything' so all she needed to take were the day's nappies when she dropped off her daughter. Yet she describes it as 'the most stressful year of my life'.

'The baby was still waking about three or four times a night and I was getting up at four in the morning to catch up on preparation and planning because you can't go in to teach and think "I will just have a bad day" because the baby has been sick everywhere. You have to go in and be professional. It was also quite a big shock going from coffee mornings with the baby to working at a much higher level than I had been at before. I don't think I was really prepared for the tiredness of doing both things.'

But the real killer was the hostility of some of her female colleagues. 'I had a male head teacher and actually I think the men were far more sympathetic than the female senior managers who felt that if you wanted to work at that level then you shouldn't bring any of your baggage in from home. Many of them had children but had taken longer off to be at home with them. It was a very conservative atmosphere and I felt they looked down on me, as if I was compromising my child's welfare and upbringing and should be at home bringing my kids up and going back to work later.

'We were asked if we wanted to do another year of the joint head of faculty because it had only been on a temporary basis anyway, and I knew I didn't want to do it because it was the worst job in the world actually. And the other person didn't want to do it; we had such a terrible experience. Even though we shared a leadership position, we were considered somehow lesser than everyone else.'

Scratch below the surface of so many women's experiences of returning to anything other than a conventional nine-to-five way of working and similar prejudices start to appear. Research into the impact of flexible working usually shows that the benefits outweigh the costs – quality and quantity of work improves – and a clear majority of employees report that flexible working has a positive effect on stress levels. Moreover, those in flexible work are often found to be more organised, committed and in some cases have higher levels of job satisfaction. One of Anne's deputy heads told her that he saw part-timers as 'very good value for money' because they did proportionately more work than full-timers and she admits that, as she worked in a local school, she would often pop in on her days off to make sure everything was sorted out for lessons on the days she would be working.

Yet many employees still opt for informal ways of working flexibly because they feel that formalising it could damage their long-term career prospects. According to the advisers at Working Families, there is some evidence that the effects of the credit crunch may now be prompting women to abandon requests for flexible work, partly because of financial pressures at home but also because they feel they need to increase their 'visibility' at work. 'The new right to ask for flexible work is not yet well embedded enough for them not to worry that they will be the first to go if there are any redundancies,' explains chief executive Sarah Jackson. Many still believe that arrangements like job-shares, term-time working and flexible hours will only become 'acceptable' when used by a wide spectrum of employees rather than just by women with young children, because that inevitably leads to assumptions about the 'type' of people who work flexibly and their levels of commitment.

Anne went back to teaching three days a week, to escape the extra pressure created by having to prove herself as a part-time worker in a leadership role.

'I had had all the rubbish from the top and all the rubbish from the bottom. The politics, the jumping through hoops, having to do things by tomorrow and having absolutely no time to myself, so I realised it wasn't worth the money or the kudos,' she says.

'It was just such an overwhelming sense of relief to give it up. I know as a part-timer that I can forget having career progression. I often teach some very challenging boys, and that does take time to manage and sort out. I still don't ever go in unprepared and will get up at four in the morning so that I don't impact the family life because a five-year-old cannot understand why Mummy is marking work and not talking to her for hours.'

The trade-off between status and income, time and peace of mind hasn't left Anne with time on her hands. Even though her children are all school age now, she has managed to fit in a Master's degree, is a chair of governors of a local primary school and is now even contemplating a PhD and a change of career to become a primary school teacher.

After Eve took her post-natal redundancy package, without even questioning whether her employers should have found her another job, she quickly got pregnant again and by the time her second son was ten months old the financial and emotional pull back to work meant she started looking for jobs again. 'I think I felt I hadn't left work on my terms and I really missed it, although the bits of work I missed may well have been the bits I couldn't actually do any more, like going to the pub and stuff. I didn't want to travel a long distance, so I found another job in a smaller publishing company closer to home and started off full-time with a nanny to care for the children while I was at work.'

For Eve, being separated from her sons for the first time was extremely difficult, and the stress was exacerbated by a fraught and unhappy relationship with one nanny who had to be sacked, a child who suffered from chronic eczema and had to be dressed in wet wraps and also taken for regular hospital visits, and a husband who offered little support. 'The job was difficult; it was a new company and a new area of work for me. I had quite a lot of responsibility and it was stimulating but at the same time I was running everywhere, from work to home and back to book launches in the evening. It was impossible to juggle everything.

'After three months in that job I went in to my boss – who I got on extremely well with, she was lovely – and said I have got this abusive nanny, it is really difficult, Tom doesn't offer me much support, and I don't feel I am doing this job well and giving you what you want. She had kids too, and she was great. She said, "Go part-time, that is fine," and she offered me a lot of admin support which is what I needed. So I went part-time and got a new nanny who was so calm, when I came home there wasn't that madness, the kids weren't hyper. But we were still up a lot in the nights and Sam was still breastfeeding as well – he breastfed until he was two, just at night because it was a comfort thing – which was exhausting. Even though I did three days and had nice long weekends, the workload was really mounting up. So things were slipping at work and I was making mistakes.'

The tipping point came when the new nanny got pregnant and her hospital visits started to eat in to Eve's work days. 'My boss started having little niggles at me and one day when an overseas author came in I left fifteen minutes before I was supposed to so the nanny could go home early. I got this really stinking email because I hadn't asked her permission. I just thought crikey, on one level I am quite senior and I have a lot of responsibility and on another level you don't trust me and you think I am skiving and of course she hadn't realised that I had shifted everything to be at the meeting. I thought the fact that she had sent the email was a bit weird; she could just have come to talk to me about it.'

By the end of that year, when the boys were three-and-a-half and two, Eve had quit her job and became the full-time mum that she never thought she would be, before her first late pregnancy. 'I just missed them dreadfully, and I loved work but I think I loved them more, and I thought maybe I should just spend a few more years at home.

'It was the first job I had ever walked away from. I feel a bit ambivalent really, a mixture of feelings. I am sad that it didn't work out for me because I really liked the company and it was good fun, but I am really glad I am with the boys. I enjoy being at home now and feel a lot more relaxed about my choices.'

Like Anne, the urge to carry on working hasn't left her and she is also planning to retrain as a primary school teacher once her own children start school.

'I have grown into the role of mum, and that was quite a shock to me, and I don't know why because I have been an auntie since

I was fourteen and I think I thought it was going to be like being an auntie, which is ridiculous. So that shocked me, and also realising how much support you need mentally and physically, I mean I was exhausted and it is only now that I can get my head above water a bit.'

Phrases like 'keeping my head above water', 'holding it all together', 'one step away from chaos' speak volumes to all of us. There aren't many working mothers who don't feel like they are drowning at some time or another in those early years, especially with more than one child, when even getting out of the house can feel like a military operation.

Having time to think through the eventual consequences of giving up a long-standing job or even fully considering the costs of scaling back and going part-time may seem as unlikely a prospect as flying to the moon when you are knee-deep in nappies, negotiating with nannies, silently raging at your surly employer or preparing work at four in the morning, but being a parent is a continuum with different needs and problems to overcome at different times. Eventually everyone surfaces for air, and new opportunities, like those that opened up for Anne, Eve and Jane, suddenly seem possible.

CHAPTER 3

Who's Minding the Baby?

My own children give a lot of credit for their apparently happy childhood to the kind, intelligent, part-time nanny who worked three days a week for us for eight years when the children were in primary school. She managed to get her own degree in the meantime, and remains a firm family friend. After one early clash over how we managed our time and precious space – when we were together in our then very small house while I was working – I came to realise that in many ways she was a better 'mother' than me, having patience for the sort of board games, puzzles and creative activities that the children loved but which always left me cold.

After she left I was obliged to rely on a neighbour who could do papier mâché and basic construction with cereal boxes for those endless school projects that required parents to help build castles and other objects. Nor did I feel in the slightest bit guilty that while Anna may have provided a good substitute for me, in some ways I could never be a good substitute for her.

In common with hundreds of thousands of other families we

also relied on what is known as 'informal' (unpaid) care. My parents always looked after the children for one day every week and it is only very recently that my now widowed mother has stopped coming round every Thursday to be there after school. Often there are no children at home when she visits and she and I will just sit on our own and have a cup of tea, or she will offer to walk the dog; the old ritual of her involvement in and commitment to our family's life is hard to shift.

But it wasn't all plain sailing. I don't think I know any working parent who hasn't had a childcare upset of some sort over the years, including me. Mine ranged from the nanny I suspected of being bulimic and whose doctors' appointments turned out to be visits to a private clinic providing diet pills, the beautiful Jehovah's Witness who was prevented by her beliefs from celebrating children's birthdays or Christmas and used to spend much of her time ironing the clothes (she borrowed from me) that she would later wear while out on her door-knocking mission, or the smart, funny young man who I thought would be good with prepubescent sons who turned out to enjoy a quick snooze on the sofa while my then (older) children played in the street outside.

Even after all my own ups and downs I am convinced that most children will survive and flourish if you have managed to create that strong bond with them in the early months and years, if the childcare is 'good enough' and your relationship with your employer allows you time to build a responsive, loving relationship with them, especially as they get older and become more selective about when they want to talk to you.

Nevertheless, the process of choosing the right childcare and the investment that parents (usually the mother) have to put into what is often a close personal and professional relationship with their children's carers is inevitably suffused with emotion, risk and bucketloads of stress. When academics from London University recently investigated the 'childcare markets' and choices made by middle-class parents in two different London boroughs, the most common word used to describe making childcare arrangements was 'nightmare'.

For many women, finding the right person to look after the kids is as much a constraint on returning to work and sustaining a demanding job as the unhelpful, bullying or unsympathetic employer. It isn't just finding the right carer, in the right place and for the right price – because cost is still a huge factor for many families – that preoccupies so many working mothers, it is also the eternal vigilance that is needed to ensure that the good quality of care that you assume you are paying for at the start is sustained over a long period of time.

While babies and small children are more resilient than they may look and are capable of forming strong, close relationships with more than one carer, chopping and changing the person who looks after them is not a good idea. Holding on to a good nanny, child-minder, or place in a good day nursery can make the first few years back at work; losing a good person or choosing the wrong arrangement can break them.

Women may have always worked but the dilemma of who should look after their children has never been as divisive and contentious as it is today. For much of human history, in agricultural and peasant communities, parents and children either worked together with offspring of all ages contributing to the family budget, or young children were looked after in group care by grandparents and older siblings. In some cultures babies are still cared for today in large stable groups of adults, and even breastfed by more than one woman, although the mother is still the primary carer.

As our own economy developed in the nineteenth century and more women moved out into domestic service or factories, younger children were cared for by friends, relatives or minders within the local community, often in a more formalised way. Local child-minding networks were relatively unregulated although there is some evidence that they came within the remit of the local health visitors. A 1930 report for one Medical Officer of Health reported on thirty-five children up to age two not cared for by their mothers; eighteen were being looked after at home by relatives, thirteen being cared for by strangers and all apparently being well looked after in good surroundings. Getting a 'bad name' as a childminder in a working-class neighbourhood was an 'awful' fate.

More affluent families had their nannies and governesses. Women whose position in society determined that they shouldn't or couldn't work had no qualms about handing over their children to substitute mothers and indeed may have been more remote from their children than many working women are accused of being today. The arrival of compulsory education during the 20th century gradually ended the parallel employment of child labour. In the last fifty years, as the extended family has become a less reliable, although still very important, source of care an affordable, universally available childcare system has lagged far behind the rapid expansion of women's work.

While the overwhelming majority of working mothers use some form of childcare, the national picture is a patchwork of different arrangements. Most families use a combination of formal childcare, such as nurseries, childminders, au pairs and nannies and informal arrangements with friends, relatives and – predominantly – grandparents.

We may not be in the same league as a country like Finland, where all childcare workers must have a Master's degree but a new Children's Workforce Development Council is seeking to ensure that all adults caring for small children have appropriate and, if possible, higher-level qualifications. This should be a time of greater reassurance about who, exactly, we are entrusting our children to. All local authorities must provide an information service for parents about registered childcare in their area and refer parents on to other agencies that can provide detailed advice about nannies and au pairs. Charities like the Daycare Trust offer a mine of information and questions to ask before you start investigating childcare options in your area. Most nurseries and childminders are now required by law to be registered and operate within a rigorous government inspection framework. Only the private nanny sector remains unregulated.

Yet nowhere is the ambivalence about whether mothers of small children should work more conspicuous than in the national hand-wringing about who should look after the baby. Are nurseries better or do they damage your child, are nannies or childminders safe, or should only mum or close relatives care for the children before they start school?

Combatants on all sides of the arguments have strong views which they will bat for forcibly, aided and abetted by interventions from the media. When I searched the Internet for the phrase 'nannies from hell' as a joke, I discovered not only a TV documentary by that name but several more with equally chilling titles such as *Nurseries Undercover* which, it turned out, many of the mothers interviewed for this book had watched.

Consumer-generated video clips alleging cruelty and mistreatment captured on parents' 'nanny cams' hidden in the home are widely available on the Internet; there was actually a storyline in the TV series *Desperate Housewives* about this. But fact is stranger than fiction in a world where parents can be caught in the crossfire of a squabble which is often remote and rooted in complex, nuanced pieces of academic research which, when distilled into one-dimensional newspaper headlines, come painfully close to home.

There are two important things to remember. First, that you can find research that backs up almost any prejudice or viewpoint – looking through the recent history of claim and counterclaim about childcare I found that very persuasive cases could be made both for and against almost any form of childcare. Within minutes of surfing the net, I found two stories, both from the same paper on different dates; one argued persuasively that nurseries 'created yobs' and another stated categorically that nurseries could 'prevent children turning into yobs'.

The second is that there is *no* reason why, with good-quality, responsive and loving care whether in a nursery, with a childminder, nanny or granny at home, your child should suffer lasting damage when you go back to work, especially if you have benefitted from a decent period of maternity leave and can arrange some flexibility in your job.

Finally you need to find the type of childcare that is right for you. The range of choices available to parents now is much greater than it was even twenty years ago when I was a new mother, and can appear baffling. The present government's National Childcare Strategy has a target of making a childcare place available to every parent who wants one by the end of the decade.

That has led to a rapid growth in the number of day nurseries, offering full- or part-time 'sessional' care to babies and very small children in nurseries that are open between 8am and 6pm. These nurseries are quite distinct from nursery schools or nursery classes attached to primary schools and which offer early education for children aged three to five.

It sometimes seems, travelling around the country, that private nurseries are popping up or being advertised everywhere. In many large urban areas, parents can choose anything from a small private nursery converted from a residential property, to nurseries set up in large office blocks, shopping centres and even sports centres. Some offer very basic no-frills provision, while others try to entice more affluent parents with luxury extras like baby yoga, organic food, cookery and gardening clubs – and even French lessons for toddlers.

The current government is committed to building a Children's Centre, offering childcare, in every community. Some of these will have links to local childminders, another vital part of the current childcare 'market'. Over 600,000 preschool-age children are looked after in some form of day-care setting.

Many mothers do now 'shop around', looking for childcare that matches their needs in terms of hours, cost, proximity and availability. Local networks of parents usually buzz with gossip about the best nurseries and childminders, and competition for places with them is often fierce.

Transport is a very real issue for some parents and carting

children, buggies and nannies off to nursery several miles away before work can seem like a job in itself. There is a world of difference between the average cost of a childminder (between £144 and £162 a week), a nursery place (between £160 to £180 a week), the top-of-the-range nurseries catering to more affluent, full-time working parents that charge up to £1,000 a month and a nanny's salary which can now top £30,000 (including tax and national insurance) in the south-east.

But in the end the decision often comes back to a personal instinct, or hunch, about what is best for your child. Some women can't face the thought of their children in nurseries simply because it feels too institutional, even if the care and facilities are superb. Others feel safer with that, and are haunted by the thought that their child might form too close a relationship with a one-to-one carer.

Even though Karen and her husband Richard live in a small village in West Yorkshire, there were a range of options open to them when she started to contemplate going back to work when their son George was five months old. As a freelance physiotherapist, she was looking for a contractual arrangement locally, to give her regular work and some flexibility, but finding the right childcare came before finding the right job.

'George is a very happy kid who had never cried when we left him with other people,' says Karen. 'We don't have a nursery in our village but there are a couple in the next town on the way to work for both of us. So I looked at two nurseries and two childminders in the area and decided virtually within a couple of days that he was more a nursery kid than a childminder kid from the way he responded when he was there, and the way he mixed with the people, so I just had a chat with them and a look around. I just liked the feel of the nursery I chose in the end. The woman who was in charge at the time just picked him up and cuddled him and he seemed completely happy and content.'

But having found the environment that felt right for her son, she had to face the dilemma of having to wait for a place.

'At the time, I was planning to go back to work a full five days a week but they didn't have a place either on a Wednesday or a Friday afternoon so I sat on it for a couple of days. But there were just so many advantages and I didn't really want to send him anywhere else so my husband and I agreed that we would simply have to find a way.'

Getting the right childcare may mean making a compromise at work. Even though Karen had planned to go back to work full-time she felt it was worth negotiating a four-and-a-half-day week and slightly less money to secure a place at the right nursery. Richard's parents agreed to look after their grandson on one day and Karen sorted out a job that allowed her Friday afternoons off. All ended well. 'I sorted out a job that I now love, working on a freelance basis for a small private company which means I only get paid for the work I do, but they are great employers and extremely flexible,' she explains.

Finding the right nursery isn't always possible, however. Rachel, a small dynamo of a woman who works a mind-bogglingly complicated shift system as a hospital consultant in South Wales, was in no doubt that a nursery was the right choice for her daughter Amy, now five, when she went back to work the first time and subsequently for her son Josh, now three.

'I just felt they were safer with a group of individuals than with only one. I felt that they would get to know more children, they would get better social interaction and there would be more people looking after them and it would be reliable. A lot of my colleagues have nannies and I know that can cause a lot of problems if the nanny phones in sick or wants time off because they have other family commitments like relatives or their own children who are ill and need looking after.

'I also worried that I wouldn't be able to get on with a nanny. I've seen that too in some of my friends, the nanny's fantastic for a year and it somehow manages to cool off until eventually everybody's sort of relieved it's ended. I know that that is not always the case, but I think that I would end up as one of those individuals, so I thought mine were better off going to nursery.'

In spite of her reservations about the personal relationship with a one-to-one carer her exacting standards about what she expected in a good nursery proved hard to meet. 'I checked out five nurseries, I wasn't happy with any of them. In fact the only one I was happy with was miles away.

'But my husband put his foot down and said it was just too far away so we chose the closest nursery on the understanding that if it was a problem we would move them and it has been fantastic. I don't know if they get enough one-to-one attention and I did worry a lot about that at the start but at the same time I know they are very happy and love going there.'

Day-care nurseries have much lower adult-to-child ratios than nursery schools or nursery classes attached to primary schools. One adult is required for every three children under the age of two, and for every four two-year-olds. Yet some of the most ferocious claims and counterclaims about the long-term effects of early childcare are focused on the quality of care in children's centres and day nurseries.

Even though it is now the childcare of choice for many women like Rachel and Karen, who both took time and trouble to investigate all the options available for their children, critics of nursery care like to paint it as cruel to children and motivated by the demands of the economy rather than of families, as women are forced back into work with no alternative but to put their children in what can sound like regimented, soulless institutional care.

The critics point, in particular, to a highly complex, long-running study carried out in the USA where there is little paid maternity leave and many women are back at work within six weeks of their children's birth. Concern about the long-term effects on a generation of children in day care led the US National Institute of Child Health and Human Development to observe the lives of 1,200 children from ten American communities from birth through to starting school.

The study's regular reports have provided a wealth of information about the effects of childcare and it is by no means all negative. Children who were looked after by well-qualified, responsive and sensitive carers in an environment where there was a good adult-child ratio tended to have better vocabularies, a more advanced attention span and memory, and better social skills. This finding has been backed up by other UK studies.

However, some children in the US study (around 16 per cent) who were in nursery or day care for thirty hours a week or longer showed some signs of difficult behaviour by the time they reached nursery school. Children who were in nursery care for less than ten hours a week showed much lower levels of problem behaviour.

This triggered what became known as the 'day-care wars' in the USA in the 1990s when a London-based American academic and psychologist, Jay Belsky, used the American survey to conclude that infants under twelve months in day care for longer than twenty hours a week risked poor attachments to their mothers and later antisocial behaviour.

In 2004 *The Guardian* writer Madeleine Bunting took up the gauntlet, backed by further evidence from the UK EPPE (Effective Provision of Pre-School Education) study, carried out by researchers at Oxford University and the Institute of Education. This had been tracking three thousand British children, to assess the benefits of early years' education. Again, it was clear that high-quality childcare and preschool education could help children do better academically but that a *small* proportion of children who had been in day care in the first two years showed signs of aggression and bad behaviour.

In an article headlined 'Are nurseries bad for our kids?' she articulated what many anxious parents were already feeling about full-time nursery care that 'instinctively it doesn't feel quite right'. That short phrase seemed to sum up the dilemma every parent has to face when deciding who should look after their children while they are at work; a dilemma in which rational choice, often based on hard evidence, becomes permeated with emotion and fear.

So should parents, contemplating going back to work and leaving their child in either a private or publicly funded nursery, panic? The answer is probably a qualified no. There are several large-scale examples of the benefits of good nursery care in the Nordic countries where many parents can share generous paid parental leave and also have access to generously subsidised, high-quality preschool care and early education and where children achieve highly and score well on many other indicators of 'well-being'.

And, even though there are some parallels between the US and UK research, British mothers are entitled to far more generous periods of paid leave after giving birth than their American counterparts. Many British mothers do go back to work part-time or with flexible working patterns or rely on friends and relatives for a mix of childcare, so children are not always in nursery care for thirty or forty hours a week.

It is also worth remembering that in all these surveys on both sides of the Atlantic, the vast majority of children (more than four-fifths in the US study) didn't display *any* behavioural problems yet were developing better language and social skills than children who were being looked after at home or by other relatives or child-minders. Around 17 per cent of four-year-olds develop signs of challenging behaviour whether they are in nurseries or not, so the study's findings simply reflect national trends.

And there is a question mark over whether a child's behaviour at four is necessarily a predictor of future delinquency, antisocial behaviour or poor mental health, since children all develop at different rates. Some of the most robust defenders of day care point out that children in nursery care often simply develop many characteristics, as well as illnesses like colds, ear infections and flu, at a faster rate than the children who don't join any sort of group care until they start school. They also note that the research doesn't show what happens to the nursery children later on, or record how their peers who have been cared for at home react once they start school. Nor does it account for the effect that parenting at home might have on both the children's academic achievement and their behaviour, even though parenting is widely agreed to be the single most important influence on how children develop.

Being a working mother faced with the news that your child is in an unsatisfactory nursery can be devastating. Julia was in the fortunate position of doing a job she liked, as a PA to two directors of a national bank in the East Midlands, when she got pregnant at forty-one and gave birth to her only child, Nathan. She put off motherhood because she and her partner, a long-distance lorry driver, felt they couldn't afford a baby when she was younger. They needed two incomes to afford the cosy terraced house they share in Nottingham and, once Nathan was born, Julia wanted to go back to work rather than live off state benefits.

But with a partner away a lot, no family nearby and unable to rely on friends with children of similar age to help out, as most of her schoolfriends had their children when much younger and many were now in secondary school or young adults, she had no choice but to depend on 'formal childcare'.

Julia, a statuesque blonde, describes her return to work as 'brilliant'. Apart from a few tears on her first day back, she settled in quickly, and everyone was delighted to see her. Nathan loved his private nursery, the cost of which was partly offset by a childcare voucher scheme which allowed Julia and her partner John to pay for their childcare out of untaxed income.

Julia had researched the childcare options in detail well in advance of going back to work, already worried by some of the allegations about day-care nurseries that had been made on television.

'It was a bit daunting because you think, I'm giving my most precious possession to this place and there are all these programmes on television about nurseries where they put cameras in without anyone knowing. I can hardly bear to watch any of them because what they say is going on in some nurseries is so awful.

'But in the end I decided I wanted him in a nursery because the chances are that he'll be an only child and I wanted him to get to play with other kids and learn to share and things like that.'

After choosing what she felt was the right nursery for her son, studying the Ofsted report and getting to know and like the staff, she got a phone call one afternoon during Nathan's third week there to tell her that the nursery had gone bankrupt and was closing down. 'I just started to cry, all the staff had lost their jobs, *they* needed to get paid at the end of that week and I had just paid almost five hundred pounds for the next month. I was incredibly lucky: the manager said to me, "I shouldn't do this but if you come now I'll give you your cheque back," so I was down there like a shot.'

Aware of the competition for good nursery places in her area, Julia was immediately on the phone to another local childcare provider, which was slightly more expensive but also recommended. The nursery was only able to offer a temporary placement while another child was on holiday. It took the family three months to get a full-time place, during which Julia and her partner were forced to take holiday and Julia's sister, who lives more than a hundred miles away, came to look after Nathan to cover the time they were both at work. When she got back to work she felt the need to prove herself even more: 'I didn't want anyone to be able to say I was not pulling my weight because I had got a child.'

The new nursery, also run by a private provider, worked well until the management announced that it was raising its fees by

25 per cent. 'I had a little cry at my desk, it was like being punched in the stomach because it meant £128 a month increase with only a few weeks' notice.'

Helped by friends at work and her employers, Julia worked out that by compressing her hours, she could go home early one day a week and save one afternoon's fees at the nursery. It was a punishing regime though, not helped by the frequent absences of Nathan's lorry-driver father.

By the time Nathan turned three, the family's routine was settled and calm. Nathan was starting to take up his entitlement to two-and-a-half hours of free early years education every day, as part of his nursery care which reduced her childcare costs. Julia felt she had cracked her childcare problems. Then the bombshell dropped. The nursery got a terrible Ofsted report, and was failed in every category. The subsequent parents' meeting was 'like an angry mob', she recalls. 'There were parents crying and some took their children out the next day.

'I felt like I had been physically punched again that day; I thought am I really being blind to all this because he just loves it there, but things had obviously slipped very quickly after the previous manager left.'

Having to decide whether or not to move a child who is otherwise happy and settled with a childminder or a nursery that may otherwise be judged failing is a dilemma most of us would rather not face. Julia plunged from feeling proud that she had managed to go back to work full-time to feeling wracked with guilt.

'I'm a bit of a planner, an organiser, that's what I do as a job I suppose, and I had planned Nathan's childcare so carefully, choosing the first nursery, going on practice runs and you know,

I'd left him for half an hour, then an hour, then I'd gone for afternoons and then left him for whole days and in the end, I took him out of one place, chucked him in another and just left him.

'I knew what he was like as a child, he's very adaptable, but I did feel very guilty, just leaving him. I've always been quite emotional but I think since I've had Nathan I'm less emotional in the sense that I haven't got time to be emotional. I've just got to sort it if I am going to be able to carry on working.'

The inspection process helped Julia to understand her rights as a parent. After the inspection she could also see that changes were being made, more experienced staff were being brought in, money was being spent on equipment and displays and more responsive communication with parents was being established. She decided to keep Nathan where he was rather than move him so soon before he was due to start primary school. She could have taken up her son's nursery education entitlement (available to all three- and four-year-olds) in a school-based nursery class, but that would have meant moving him for two-and-a-half hours in the middle of the day. Above all, she could see that he was happy both in the nursery and at home and she felt his behaviour and learning weren't suffering.

Recognising that the quality of care in a nursery may not be good enough can be tricky for parents who simply drop off and pick up, especially if the children seem happy. The chances are that if you choose a nursery for your child, it won't be failing – the most recent report from the government's watchdog Ofsted looked at over eighty thousand childcare and early years settings in England between 2005 and 2008 and concluded that nearly two-thirds of day-care nurseries were good or outstanding, around a third were satisfactory and a very small proportion were not good enough. Scotland, Wales and Northern Ireland have different regulation systems which allow parents to see inspection reports for individual care settings. However, there is *nothing wrong* with taking an active, healthy interest in what happens while you are at work, whether your children are in a nursery, with a childminder or at home with a nanny. Just walking out the door and hoping everything will be all right, especially if your heart tells you it isn't, won't work in the long run. I know because I have done it from time to time in that battle against 'the unforgiving minute' but I have always regretted it later. There is plenty of information out there and clear standards against which you can judge the quality of care your child is receiving.

In a good or outstanding nursery, children should be safe, happy, being stimulated and above all being cared for by well-trained staff with a low adult-to-child ratio.

Knowing that your children will be safe is probably the highest priority for most parents and a good or outstanding nursery or childminder would have careful staff-vetting procedures and clear child-protection procedures in place and be vigilant about the child-staff ratios being maintained.

'One of the comments that most upset me in the inspection report at my son's nursery was the one that said children were allowed to hurt each other,' explains Julia. 'The staff seemed to have lost direction. The manager who was there when I first went in was very supportive. She was an ex-Ofsted inspector but when she left the morale obviously went through the floor. They'd lost direction on things like the toilet rota, so three children wanted the toilet, and three adults took them so there was one adult left with too many children.'

Quality of leadership is obviously crucial to a well-run nursery. Once the leadership starts to fail, all sorts of other management problems can follow. Asking about how the staff are supported, trained and the rate of staff turnover is a very legitimate question, as are questions about first-aid procedures, how many accidents the nursery has every year, whether they have a 'key worker' system so that every child or baby has a named person who is responsible for him or her and for feeding back information to parents.

Staff should be able to recognise signs of abuse, carry out regular risk assessments and be able to help children develop a sense of personal and road safety and, of course, ensure that children can't wander in and out of the premises unnoticed. We have all seen the stories of the toddler who found his or her way out to a busy road or, in very rare incidences, been injured by inadequate or negligent staff.

Nurseries or childminders who fail this spectacularly make disproportionately prominent headlines. But examples like these are very rare. In the 2008 Ofsted Chief Inspector's report only 2 per cent of childcare settings were judged unsafe and of these most were served with enforcement notices to improve, or risked losing (or lost) their registration.

Julia was also shocked to learn that in Nathan's nursery, which was run by a large multinational chain of childcare providers, the children's observation folders were empty and parents had never been offered the six-monthly consultation evening with staff to which they were entitled.

A good nursery would have a combination of structured play and learning activities which are fun but also stimulating, as well as a routine that allows small children or babies to rest or sleep.

Nurseries and carers who pay attention to encouraging children to talk, listen, look at books and work with each other, developing social skills and self-confidence through well-structured and organised activities, can give young children a huge head start before their move to more formal education. In the small number of examples where this isn't done adequately, children are often unstimulated and bad behaviour can follow.

Nurseries are also now expected to help children to understand what 'being healthy' means. This doesn't just mean being given fresh, healthy, wholesome food but also requires them to be physically active, visiting outdoor parks, riding bikes, dancing and playing games and being watchful for children becoming ill. This can cause problems for working parents if sick children need to be kept off or taken home.

When Sangita started her new job four months into her maternity leave, she managed to get her son into a highly recommended local nursery which fitted all her needs.

'I knew people I really respected who had been there, it had a nice big garden and obviously as we lived in a flat with a small garden, that felt like a real advantage for Manish. It is an old-fashioned council nursery where you know there is good supervision, lots of people on duty, they have training sessions once a week and they give the children fruit snacks. My sister has just put her kid in nursery and they give him a KitKat at snack time so I feel quite relieved that they didn't do that at mine.'

She had several falling-outs with the nursery over illness, however. 'When he first went he was sick all the time which was hideous because they kept calling me, and I was a month into a new job and having to go home several days a week to take him out.

Perhaps rather cruelly I kept just saying he is not really ill, he had just got a temperature, can't you just give him some Calpol and he will be fine, and they would be quite rude and refuse because they weren't allowed to give Calpol in the nursery. I had an ongoing battle about it but once that kind of sickness phase passed he started sleeping and he was fine.

'I did feel conflicted, of course. We don't really have huge amounts of family close by so it was hard. There were times when he was sick and I would have to call my mum and ask her to get him, which is an hour-and-a-half's journey for her, or my husband, who has been in his job for quite a while, would have his fair share of getting out of work.'

The most common alternative type of registered formal childcare is to use a childminder. Anyone who now looks after children in their own home, for payment, should be registered as a childminder. Over 300,000 children are looked after by childminders in the UK. Guidelines as strict as those for nurseries govern the numbers of children a childminder can look after. One childminder should care for no more than six children under eight, with no more than three children under five. Of those three, only one child should be under a year old.

New mother Emma investigated all the local registered childcare options before she was due to start her new job in Cambridge after the birth of her first daughter. She researched all the inspection reports and spoke to other local parents in the mother and toddler group she used, eventually deciding that a nursery wasn't right for her.

'I started off speaking to my mum who has worked in childcare services for a long time. She is a great supporter of childminders for young children, rather than day care, but we still looked at three nurseries and three childminders and in the end I really liked the idea of a childminder. I felt it was less institutionalised when the children were so young. I think there are some very good nurseries, but it seemed just more kind of normal really, for the children to be in someone's home where they can go out and about but are in an environment that's, well, homely I suppose.

'The other thing I liked was the idea of continuity of care. Edie has had the same husband-and-wife team looking after her from nine months, so it's not like every year or every six months in a nursery they go up to the next room and someone else is looking after them. Also, siblings go as well so when I go back to work after this maternity leave, my son and daughter will be there together. It is quite a big house and they won't be in separate rooms in the same place. But most relevant of all is that they got an outstanding Ofsted rating, so we are just very lucky.'

Childminders are inspected in much the same way as nurseries. They all have to be registered, are also required to be insured, have first-aid training, be checked by the Criminal Records Bureau, have some training and provide a safe, stimulating, healthy environment for the children in their care.

The advantage of leaving children in a childminder's home is that it does feel more intimate and personal than a large nursery. But some parents don't like the idea that their children might form a close relationship with one carer, and using a childminder can also present logistical difficulties if you can't find someone good close to your own home.

For mothers like Beverly, after she came through her post-natal depression, moved back to England and started looking for jobs following a lengthy career break, a childminder seemed like the perfect solution. Her eldest daughter was in school and her younger son still of preschool age and Beverly felt the childminder would provide a warm, homely after-school atmosphere for her daughter. But eventually she found that the travelling involved in dropping off and collecting the children proved insurmountable.

'I was getting up at 6am and was permanently exhausted. It took me an hour to take Charlotte to school and then come back to pack my son's bag, make his food then drive him to the childminder who also picked my daughter up from school. So I would leave him and he'd be absolutely hysterical and I would feel hysterical because I felt he wasn't having a nice time, and I didn't want to leave him in that kind of state. Then I would get there in the evening and he'd be crying again, and she'd say he'd been unhappy all day.

'And there were other issues – for example if my son was sick or the other children the childminder was looking after were sick it was a nightmare. I would wake up for work and think, "Am I actually going to make it in today?" because babies are ill all the time. That's why we went for the nanny option.'

For many mothers, if their own families can't step in to help, the next best thing to having your children at home with you is to have them at home with a nanny. There are many high-profile supporters of the view that having a nanny is the best alternative to full-time maternal care. Indeed the 'nanny's best' argument is wheeled out as regularly as the 'nurseries creates yobs' stories.

Childcare expert Penelope Leach came down firmly in favour of mothers using nannies when she headed a child development study of 1,200 children in the UK which suggested that the social and emotional progress of children under three cared for in nurseries, by childminders or even relatives, could be impaired.

She was quickly forced to qualify the findings when the inevitable headlines like 'Mother's care best for children' followed pointing out that she didn't mean to suggest that every child in a large nursery would 'become a monster' or that all mothers should 'stay at home and give up work'. Leach even admitted that some mothers may not be the best people to care for their children if they are depressed or simply don't enjoy long periods at home with them, but she still maintained her support for nannies in the home.

Psychologist and author Oliver James took a similar position in his book *Affluenza*, which suggests that the pursuit of wealth, money and even fame has left women vulnerable and devalued mothering.

'It impels them and their partners to buy property they cannot afford, creating a perpetual sense of impoverishment, almost however rich they are, and putting them under pressure to work whilst their children are small,' he wrote. 'It encourages them to regard only paid work as a source of self-esteem … above all it makes them and their society downgrade the huge importance of caring for small children – almost everywhere I went, the role of mother had a status somewhat lower than that of street-sweeper.'

One of the 'vaccines' James prescribes to combat the modern-day virus of affluenza is to avoid day care and always choose nannies as the 'least worst' form of substitute care if you *must* go back to work.

Nanny care is certainly different from being cared for either in a nursery or someone else's home, but may not necessarily be better. There are good and bad nannies just as there are good and bad nurseries and childminders. As with all other types of childcare, the long-term impact on your child is inevitably moderated by a number of other factors as well as quality; how much time children spend with their carer, their age and the sort of parent you are at home.

One nanny fact is irrefutable though. They can be very expensive. The £30,000 a year charged by some nannies in the southeast of England (and around three-quarters of Britain's nannies are in the south-east) is often expected to be part of a more generous package which can include sole use of a car, self-contained accommodation and expensive foreign holidays. The graduate 'super nanny' can now earn more than a newly qualified nurse or primary school teacher.

In Beverly's case, the high cost of a sole nanny was mitigated by finding a 'share' with another family in what sounds like a fiendishly complicated arrangement but is also one that works for the family.

'I work two full days and one afternoon from home,' explains Beverly. 'The nanny looks after the children on the days when I am at work. She comes at eight and she takes my daughter to school, and then looks after my son, picks my daughter up from school, does the homework and things like that until I get home about 6.30. She also looks after them at home on the days I am working there and it works out really well. It is only just now, since we've had a nanny and particularly since my son has been looked after in his own home, that everything has fallen into place with work.'

Finding the right nanny to suit the budget of an average family with two working parents is still hard.

'I did tell the agency who found her that I had a limited budget which meant at first I was looking at people who were relatively inexperienced, either coming from jobs in a nursery or people who had children of their own,' says Beverly. 'The first nanny had her own daughter but that was an issue again, because she was great with my children but if hers was ill or mine weren't feeling very well, she was reluctant to take them and she also just found it really stressful having the three kids. So I went back to the agent and he found me this nanny that I've got now. She's an experienced nursery nurse, who wanted to get into nannying, so she's got all the experience, just never been a nanny before.

'She's really sensible, a very genuine person, and the children absolutely love her so I feel totally comfortable leaving her with them because I can see their reaction to her when she comes, they kind of attack her and she's fun too. It makes it easier for me to come to work so everything has slotted into place and it is only slightly more expensive. With the old arrangement, by the time I had paid for the school holidays and for my daughter being picked up from school and fed, and then my son's whole day with the childminder, it worked out about ten pounds a day less.'

However, nannies remain the least regulated of all forms of childcare and their performance as 'substitute mothers' is not easily evaluated because they are a disparate group and often join families on a word-of-mouth recommendation. Even Penelope Leach admitted to being 'staggered' by the number of families who failed to check out references.

When Eve finally went back to her job in publishing after having her two sons, hiring a nanny was the only answer because her husband was not keen on nursery care. 'He said the children would be in schools before long and he wanted them cared for at home in the early years, even though her salary virtually wiped out my wages. But she was awful – I thought she was ideal for the kids because she was young and gregarious and she came as a recommendation from the nanny group I knew, but she was verging on abusive actually.

'I realised it when I saw Joe standing against a wall wringing his hands when she arrived. She lasted nine weeks but even in those nine weeks the initial moments of leaving to go to work were so awful I can't talk about it, even now, and they were awful because of her.

'My husband did recognise that there was a problem but he was giving me a lot of grief about it too, even though he wanted the nanny and knew that I might have felt more comfortable with them in a nursery because I thought they would have been together in a much safer environment.'

It was only after Eve sacked the nanny that she ran into someone else locally who had also employed her and experienced similar problems. 'I just thank God she wasn't in their lives for very long but she still works around here, even though some of us have tried to warn other families. The trouble with nannies is that they can be police checked but there is no national database, and if you do have concerns, who can you go to about it?'

There are many wonderful nannies, of course. I found one in the end. But if relationships between the children and the nanny start to break down they often do so in private, in a way that would be unlikely to happen in a good nursery. The informal way in which many nannies move from job to job makes it difficult to spot problems in advance and often lulls parents into thinking they will be reliable, competent and caring simply because they have worked in someone else's house and will be taking care of their own children in a familiar environment. Since 2000, nanny agencies have been obliged to take up references, carry out police checks and validate

CVs of potential candidates but that leaves thousands of nannies still unregulated if they come through personal recommendations or small ads.

Using an agency adds an extra cost but it should bring reassurance. Amanda Coxen, franchise director of Tinies, one of the country's largest nanny agencies, says that most parents who want to hire a nanny do want someone with experience and qualifications, a clean criminal record and driving licence.

'If parents go through an agency to find a nanny, then they must ask the agency if they carry out all relevant checks, which should include a Criminal Records Bureau (CRB) Enhanced Disclosure, an identity check, which would be sight of the nanny's passport, driving licence, and proof of address.

'We would also check previous employment history, which means going through the CV with the nanny, asking about each job, what the nanny did for each job, why the nanny left, as well as asking about any gaps in the history on the CV. We would do verbal checks on employment references as we feel that you can only really learn about a person by talking to the people the nanny worked for and ask to see all original childcare qualification certificates.

'Parents should also ask if the agency personally interviews all of its candidates. That I would say is the bare minimum. Having established experience and qualifications, then the two most important things after that are personality and bond with the children. Only the family can say what personality would fit in their home and what personality would work best when looking after their children. We encourage parents to call all previous employers.'

Gaps in potential nannies' CVs should also be probed. Amanda Coxen's agency always asks the nanny to explain the gap. 'If they say they went travelling, then we ask to see their passport; if they say they took time off, then we ask if they signed up for benefits, and ask to see evidence of that. By personally interviewing nannies you get to ask them direct questions and see how they respond. If there is any reason to doubt their answers, then you would not proceed with that nanny.'

Lisa, a tall, elegant mother of three, who gave up her career in a large public affairs company with a view to starting a family, admits to paying insufficient attention to the process of recruiting some of the nannies who looked after her two older children. She employed a nanny after she realised that trying to look after her first child herself, while working as a PR consultant from her Surrey home, travelling up to London for meetings, wasn't working.

'I did allow myself a bit of maternity leave, but I never said "Right that is it, I am not going to work for six months". I was always able to pick up the phone and write a proposal over a weekend or something, so I kept my hand in. I felt sure that I would manage without permanent childcare with my mother helping out but nothing prepared me for trying to cope with the baby.

'You have to be so disciplined about choosing your hours and time if you work from home. I used to try and work whenever he slept or at night but he was a nightmare baby and never wanted to sleep. I used to wonder if that was because I was always trying to put him down. I used to do most of my work at night and was going to bed at about three in the morning.

'I would go to the office occasionally but in practice it was stressful and exhausting. There were occasions, if I had a really important meeting and had to travel to get to it, that my husband would just take the day off, calling in and saying he was sick. It was very much a means to an end. My husband was also working full-time, as an insurance underwriter, but we were quite hard up in those days and I was definitely earning more money than him so we didn't really have a choice.'

Many of Lisa's friends locally were going back to full-time jobs but eventually she found another local mum who was happy to be paid to do some childcare, an arrangement that lasted until after her second son was born and she was offered a job setting up the PR and marketing department for a new company.

'It was a huge decision, and I kept breastfeeding for as long as I could; I would feed him in the morning and as soon as I got home. I did it because I needed some more stability. I think I got to the point where the juggling was exhausting me. The offer came along and they agreed to a four-day week and it meant I was formalising my child-care, and because the first carer got offered a super job we found our first nanny. Nurseries were not really an option for me because I just hated the idea. I had seen documentaries on television where they take your baby from you and they are to-ing and fro-ing all the time.'

Their first nanny had basic childcare qualifications but no paid experience and was the daughter of the friend of another local mum, so it was hard to verify references. 'When you are desperately looking for somebody and you have already seen two or three, you just end up taking the best of the worst, I mean everyone wants the ideal nanny or au pair but it doesn't always work out, and she turned out to be a complete nightmare.

'I did pick up from the kids that things weren't right, they started to get anxious about not wanting us to leave in the morning and they would get upset about getting into her car even though we would do our best to reassure them.'

The tipping point came when she got home from work to find her three-year-old son's hands covered in plasters. He had been left alone to roam around the house and managed to get a razor out of the bathroom cabinet. 'We dismissed her in the end after six months but it was horrific. She tried to get us for unfair dismissal but we managed to settle and she just walked out. It was an awful time.

'I was commuting for about two hours every day. I didn't get the time off work to deal with it all and my then employers weren't very understanding. I had only just started and I had told them it would be easy for me to be there and work, so they felt I should be dealing with it in my own time when I wasn't working. None of them had children and I was the oldest member of staff. When I look back I think how could I ever have let her into our house, but you just have to trust them initially, but I am still amazed that you can invite these people into your home and then they do something like that to you.'

Many of Lisa's problems would have been avoided if she had either gone through a well-established, reputable agency or delved into the background of her employees herself, although that can be difficult to do if they come from a local recommendation.

'I do sometimes wonder if I should simply have stayed at work from the start. I would probably have got a good package of maternity leave and some flexible working which would have allowed me to get into a proper routine with a good, experienced nanny early on. I do think I would have stayed there, I would have tried to get a better nanny and I would have been in a position to pay for a really good one.'

Another advantage of going through an agency is that mothers usually get a short probationary period during which, if the relationship breaks down or the nanny leaves, parents can either get a refund or a free replacement.

Amanda Coxen's agency issues all parents with a model contract of employment which they should complete with the nanny. 'Having a contract is a statutory requirement but also helps to set out exactly what the terms of employment are,' she explains. 'We also encourage parents and nannies to agree a job description in advance to avoid problems later. For example, we did have a nanny who started a job and then a week into it she was handed two sheets of A4 paper with additional cleaning duties/household duties the family also now expected her to do. Needless to say that placement did not work out. We also offer parents and nannies a free legal helpline, to help iron out any employment issues they may have.'

Of the two subsequent nannies Lisa employed, only one settled and became a much-loved member of the family who Lisa says 'restored my faith in childcare to a degree'. But the third was another 'nightmare', a young girl who wasn't supposed to but did frequently bring her own baby with her to work and took to picking up Lisa's two children from school, then going round to her boyfriend's and leaving the boys and her own baby in the car outside.

'The boys were old enough to tell us about it but I had no other option but to put up with it. I just felt anxious all the time and, when I got to work, was so busy I could push that out of my mind. I feel like that is a terrible thing to say but it was a relief that the children were at school for most of the time I was at work and that she was only with them for about three-and-a-half hours a day.'

Eventually both mother and nanny reached a tipping point. The nanny claimed her doctor had ordered her to stop work because of stress and Lisa realised she was secretly glad to get rid of her. But the years of juggling work and childcare finally took its toll and Lisa admits that her decision to try for another baby after a ten-year gap was 'almost a way out'.

Even though she could have taken maternity leave from her final job, working for a large IT company, she took a conscious decision to do things a different way. 'We just said if we are going to have another baby there is no point doing what we did before. Let's just enjoy this one. It really was like starting all over again. I was there to breastfeed him and there for the other two when they came home from school and needed help with their homework. I didn't have the money hanging over my head or the sense that I should be somewhere else. It was just like suddenly we were a happy family.'

Since then she has employed six au pairs, young men and women who usually come from European Union countries to study English, live in a family's home and must work for at maximum five hours a day, be given appropriate time off and provided with food, an allowance and their own room. The government's Sure Start website advises parents against using au pairs as childcare for preschool-age children since they are not trained. But they can be the perfect solution for older, school-age children especially with a parent who is working from home as they often don't stay long.

'Children have to be a certain age to take an au pair,' says Lisa. 'Some of mine were fabulous but you do have to spend time giving them an induction and taking them here, there and everywhere and writing up notes for them and listing suppers, and before you know it they are off and you have to do the same for the next one.'

There are so many 'what ifs' along the way for working mothers. It is often easy, with the benefit of hindsight, to look back and wonder if it might have been better to use a nursery or a child-minder or sack that lousy nanny earlier. The thread running through every single description or inspection criteria of 'high-quality child-care' is the nature of the relationships between the children and the adults we are entrusting them to.

There is an element of 'risk' in leaving your child with a complete stranger whether it is a childminder, a nursery nurse and someone caring for them in your own home. If those relationships are good, carers are well trained, experienced and communicate well with both parents and children, there shouldn't be a problem. But it is also easy to become defensive and reluctant to admit to anxieties about the person caring for your children especially if that involves having a difficult conversation with your employer, as Lisa found out when her new bosses expected her to sort things out in her own time.

Admitting to childcare problems in the office often feels like a sign of weakness and we have all worried about that dim view that colleagues and employers may take of parents who want time off to deal with family issues. When the Open University interviewed women of all ages and backgrounds before and after they had their children, about how they reacted to becoming mothers, many of the interviewees who worked were very resistant to the idea that motherhood would change them and could mean a loss of career.

A year later, most admitted quite profound changes in the way they felt about themselves and their positions in the world. Many were back at work but the extent to which they found themselves forced to pretend they hadn't changed depended on how malleable, interested and accepting their employers were. Some talked of almost having to pretend they weren't mothers when they were at work.

But you will never know how your employer might react to an honest request for time off to deal with a crisis at home unless you ask, and you might be pleasantly surprised. Any parent who has been in a job for a year is entitled to unpaid leave – up to thirteen weeks until their child is five. If the answer is no, there is always that other hidden goldmine – the local community. Whether it is the grannies, other mothers, friends or neighbours, they are often the lifeline when the children are ill, the nanny doesn't turn up or the electricity pylon blows down and the nursery is shut. Maintaining those relationships can be hard but they are often the secret weapon in the working mother's armoury.

CHAPTER 4

The Playground

After I had my first son, I remember being asked by one old acquaintance whether I had made a 'friend for life' with other new mothers, a bond forged through having had children at the same time. And there were other women I had met in the antenatal group, the post-natal ward, the local playground and one o'clock club who, at the time, felt like friends for life. Over time, though, returning to work stretched some of those common bonds to breaking point.

Motherhood inevitably changes the way we feel about ourselves. The outside world sees you differently, a whole new range of hitherto unknown practical tasks descend and for the first time you have another being who is solely dependent on you. It also often increases our need to be part of a local community, the demands we make and the extent to which we depend on family, friends and neighbours.

For a while, in the immediate aftermath of giving birth, the comfort zone is with other women in the same situation and the old life at work can seem curiously alien. Over time, as returning to work becomes a financial necessity or simply offers a chance to refind that old self, a subtle distinction can start to appear between the women who work and who feel confident enough to admit that simply being a mother isn't enough for them and those who don't, with hidden assumptions on both sides occasionally bubbling to the surface. As well as pretending you don't have children when you are at work, you may feel you have to pretend you don't really have a job when you are in your 'home zone' – especially if your local network is made up of other mothers who may have made different choices and may feel jealous or insecure in their decisions.

Former charity executive Karen Mattison, co-founder of the social enterprise Women Like Us, which coaches women who have been out of work after having children and helps place them in flexible jobs, thinks women are often tormented by the fantasies they have about other women's lives.

'There is one mum friend I see at school every Tuesday when I drop the boys off and race to work, usually stressed and late for a meeting. I see her in her tennis gear with another mum going off to play tennis and have coffee. I saw her this weekend and told her that every Tuesday I wish I was her and she said she sees me in my work clothes and wishes she was me!'

Admitting those secret fantasies about other women's lives being somehow better can be hard; disguising them, or allowing resentment to ferment, can rupture friendships temporarily. In the early years of being a new mother I went to stay with my oldest and closest friend, with our partners and nine-month-old sons. It ended with tears and recriminations. We had got pregnant at the same time and given birth to boys within a week of each other and thereafter taken very different paths. She had given up her full-time job for suburban life. I was then still determinedly sticking with my full-time job on a daily newspaper.

In the space of a searingly hot week of what felt like imprisonment in her spacious kitchen our friendship temporarily broke down as we both found ourselves fiercely defending our positions.

In her case this appeared to me to be a determination to prove that she was a better mother (her son ate perfect food at the right time, slept through the night and so on) while I went to great lengths to prove that she had sacrificed her professional identity to live the bleak routine of a Stepford wife. I, on the other hand, was forging the new frontier of working motherhood and had a blissfully chilled-out baby who ate usually the wrong food, was permanently covered in it, breastfed on demand all night, slept in our bed and was generally a more laid-back, happier child – something I was by no means sure of in my heart just as, I later discovered, she was tormented by what she had given up.

We laugh about it now but I have no doubt that today many women are somewhere on the continuum at each end of where we had staked out our positions. Managing those friendships is another balancing act because we need our networks of support, not just in the early years but particularly once children start school. It can be very lonely doing it all alone if you have a partner who can't help out much, or you are a lone parent.

Emma was friendly with most of the mums on her road before she had children and started going to a coffee morning with them when she was pregnant. 'I was quite surprised by the number of women who hadn't gone back to work. I didn't feel they judged me for making that choice. There have been a few comments because

Edie is quite clingy when I'm around and people have said that's probably because she doesn't see much of you so she is probably clingier when you are here. But I think if you are comfortable with your choices you can't necessarily expect everyone that you meet to agree with you and we do all meet regularly, share babysitting and even go out together regularly while the dads look after the kids.'

For others it can become a barrier to future friendship. Sangita started going back to her casework and meetings as a local councillor when her son was a few weeks old and then back to work when he was four months old. She felt a strong sense of disapproval from the mothers she had met, and got on perfectly well with, during her pregnancy.

'I had done some antenatal classes, which to be fair were very useful for the whole birth thing, but the group of women I went through that with were yummies, and slightly fascist. I remember another friend saying to me be very careful, once you are buddies with these people you will be stuck with them for years. They couldn't believe it when I started going back to council meetings when he was just a few weeks old. I remember we met up once when the babies were about eight weeks old and one of them said to me it was the first time she had got out of the house and I thought she was mad, because I couldn't wait to get out.'

In the end the friendships petered out because Sangita felt more comfortable with the mums at her son's nursery, most of whom worked. 'They were a bit more normal, and got the whole hideous juggling thing, and understood me asking the nursery just to give him some Calpol so I didn't have to come and pick him up, even though I knew that I should be just taking him straight home and tucking him up in bed.'

The divisions may appear less pronounced in smaller towns or semi-rural areas than in large urban areas where people move regularly and where communities can become more fractured and polarised by class and income. Tessa and her husband took a conscious decision to leave their metropolitan life and her civil service job to move to a small village in the Home Counties once their children were born. 'One of the reasons we left was when I had my first baby I joined the National Childbirth Trust and met up with a lot of other similar professional women,' Tessa explains. 'We would meet up again after the children were born, go to the park and the one o'clock club and there would be whole families there that we would never talk to, and I thought why are we not being friends with those people and it was like a self-selected thing, and I didn't like it.

'They didn't meet the other women or know any of them; they felt that if they came to the park with you, then they didn't want to talk to that woman over there on the swing with her kid. There was no reason to make any friends. I was so desperate for fresh blood.'

Moving to a rural community was a shock, but ultimately provided her with a network that supported a return to work in Whitehall and then on through several other less demanding jobs in the voluntary sector closer to home. 'There was absolutely no overlap between my job and my life at home and nobody in my community ever asked much about what I did. They just thought I had gone to work but they never asked about what I do as a job. It wasn't a big deal really, but they all rallied round to help.

'There were moments when the au pair would ring me at work and say your daughter won't get out of bed after her afternoon nap and I need to go out to collect the boys from school so what should I do? That was stressful for sure because I was miles away but I always knew that there was someone else close by that she could ring and get to pick up the boys. I couldn't have survived without other people helping me out with favours. If I wasn't there, I always knew someone else would be able to pick up my children so I never had to worry they would be left at the school gate.'

For some women, it takes much longer to readjust. Angela, who loathed being away from her new baby so desperately that she gave up her job in the pharmaceutical industry to move to a cheaper, more rural, part of East Anglia in order to be with her, felt out of sync with former work colleagues once she had become a mother, but also felt mismatched to her new life.

'I found it very difficult when I was working because I was neither one thing nor the other. The people who had babies at the same time as me all stuck together, and had coffee once or twice every week, which I couldn't join in with. So they'd obviously be chatting about things and seeing their babies' progress and then once I was back at work I could only come along every so often, so I felt a bit left out.

'But I would only occasionally see my work friends socially because I had a baby. That made me feel horrible, because I felt nobody wanted me, but people probably did get fed up with asking me out and then hearing me refuse because I didn't want to leave the baby. I found that hard because I wasn't here or there really.'

Even in her new environment, working from home with her children close by, the grass occasionally still seemed greener on the other side. 'Now I have moved to a new area and based at home, I'm in that place that all those other mums were when I was stuck at work, but I find I miss my work colleagues and the conversations I could have with them.

'I went to some of the mother and toddler groups here at first but to be honest they weren't my cup of tea. I wouldn't want to put any of them down and I don't mean this in a nasty way but I had been in quite an intellectual environment and shifting away from that to people who only knew about how to bring up their children was hard. The first toddler group I went to, I sat there and tried to talk to some of the women, a lot of whom were quite young mums or childminders and in the end I got a piece of paper and wrote to my colleagues back at work and said, "I'm sitting here trying to talk to people and no one wants to talk to me." But that could have been me not being very approachable?

'Eventually I found a group of friends who weren't just talking about babies so I settled down. I did have to remind myself that I could still be at work, but that I never really wanted to do that, and that getting this time I wanted with my daughter was special.'

Recent research into changing patterns of family life suggests that there may be strong but subtle regional differences in the way different communities view mothers returning to work. In her book *Rethinking Families*, sociologist Fiona Williams suggests that local culture, regional differences and economic history affect views on what it means to be a 'good' mother or father and how people ought to behave when they have children. The differing views often have roots much further back in time and may even override the rural/urban divide and class or professional background. So in some parts of the country with a long history of working women and where men's wages are low, such as the Lancashire mill towns, or South Wales, it is much more common for women to return to work full-time. By contrast, the Home Counties and East Anglia have much lower numbers of women returning to work full-time.

For Nicky, the community around her home town in South Wales has allowed her to work almost consistently since her son was born. Now living in a detached house on a sleepy estate in a small village outside Cardiff, she jokes that she and her friends, some of whom still don't have children, have 'job-shared' her son Jake. She believes that he has grown up to be a very happy and secure child thanks to his large extended 'family', many of whom are not blood relatives but who helped her back into work and into a new career rather than live on state benefits. Nicky faced life as a lone parent after she became pregnant in the third year of her nurse's training and her relationship with her son's father broke down.

'I had Jake when I was in my early twenties and had intended to go back but the circumstances were terrible. I got very down about the relationship I was in so I didn't go back for about a year and a half, because I was off sick and I just couldn't cope.

'Then a light just came on and I thought, what on earth am I doing? I knew I had to get out of the situation so I contacted the school of nursing and said I was feeling much better and wanted to come back. By then the qualification had changed so I had to pass the new exams but it made me feel much better. I finished with Jake's dad because things just weren't getting any better and I started working nights because that made it easier to find someone to look after Jake.'

That was the start of more than a decade of steady career progression which eventually took her into a new career selling medical equipment and training health professionals, entirely supported by juggling help from her parents, her grandmother and then different friends after her parents moved abroad. She only had one brief period of formal paid childcare when she employed an au pair. That came to an unhappy end when she returned from work unexpectedly and found the au pair upstairs asleep in bed while her three-year-old son watched TV on his own downstairs.

'I started out by buying a house near a friend of mine who lived in a different part of Cardiff. She looked after him for a while during the day then she had to move, so I did nights and my mum looked after him. I literally relied on friends most of the time. There was another nurse who moved into our spare room after the au pair left and we used to juggle our shifts. Otherwise, he would go to a different friend's house or to my grandmother's.

'I eventually bought a house in the next village to my grandmother and I used to take him there around eight in the evening and put him to bed, go to work, get back in time to get him ready for school then I would go home and be in bed by about a quarter past nine and get about six hours' sleep before I got him from school. He probably slept out more than he slept at home but it was always with the same select few. I would never leave him with anybody I didn't know and in the holidays he would always fly out to the Middle East to stay with my parents. I have been really lucky, but then he has been such a good child people don't mind.'

Kate's thirteen-year career as a working mother, department head in a large secondary school, would have been impossible without the support she had from her in-laws nearby.

'In my first job my in-laws, who lived in the next village, looked after my daughter four days a week. I had no outside childcare. It was fantastic, I mean the relationship my elder daughter has with my parents-in-law is just superb. When she was ill I didn't have to phone in sick to look after her. I did have to drop her off at their house, which added extra time to the journey, after she had been

fed and changed and that is not exactly like just dropping everything and leaving the house, but I wanted to make sure I wasn't
leaving them with so much extra work. We bought a double set of
equipment, a buggy and car seat and clothes and bottles, basically
all of the stuff, so the only thing I had to pack really was nappies.

'And they were very young, only around forty-five when they
first started looking after the children. My father-in-law was brilliant; he used to paint with my daughter, take her out for walks,
although they would also watch quite a bit of telly.

'It wasn't so much that we didn't want to pay for childcare, I
just felt the family was best because they have those natural ties to
the child because they have that love and that extra bond. However,
there are downsides to family looking after your children. You are
much closer and you live in their pockets far more, and yes you have
to put up with the minutiae of family life and discussing everything
with them to the nth degree, but the bonuses far outweigh that. I
was brought up by my grandmother, so for me it was very natural
to have grandparents looking after my own children.'

Not everyone is lucky enough to have family, enduring community links or lifelong friendships to rely on either for full-time care,
or simply as a buffer when things go wrong. There is a world of
difference between having a baby in the area where you grew up,
as Nicky did, especially if it is a small community with a local
culture of working mothers, and having a baby in the middle of a
big city to which you may have moved for work. When you have
been working full-time before the baby is born, it is easy to feel
frozen out in the street, playground or in the drop-in centre to
which everyone else has been going to regularly, as they will all
know each other well. In some urban areas we have got out of the

habit of talking to our neighbours, especially in mixed communities with highly mobile populations.

But in many residential neighbourhoods, well-organised family/parents support groups do exist, often with a small annual charge, that provide regular newsletters, websites, members' contact boards, information about nurseries, childminding, babysitting, community activities, other local services, nearly new sales and local events. The trick is to find out about them. Look for information in your local library, doctor's surgery, and *talk to other mothers*, however exclusive and cliquey the well-established groups may feel.

Eve's decision to give up her full-time job in publishing was partly guided by the pull back to that domestic network of friends and other mothers. She and her husband had moved from a small flat in inner London to a more residential area further out after she was initially made redundant. She had very quickly been introduced to a local parents group. 'I joined immediately and that opened up a whole new avenue through which I met a network of mothers around here who were stay-at-home mums. We all had our first children together and then we were all pregnant with our second at the same time.

'I thought I was becoming bored with it once I did finally go back to work, but once I was at work I really missed it. Even when I was at work the other mums helped me out and weren't resentful at all. Also because I worked part-time I could always help them out on my days off. I tried not to lean on them too much and also eventually I found a great nanny. That network is still really important, especially because I have no family to help me out.'

Our next-door neighbours have become like a second family but I don't think I exchanged a word with them in the first six months after we moved in, even though I had two small children, because I was preoccupied, working part-time and writing a book. Once I had a new baby a new relationship developed. Even though Victoria was then a 'stay-at-home mum' (in fact the only one I knew), we both worked out a mutual respect for each other's choices; she always kept a beady eye on my more itinerant nannies and carers and the children regularly stayed over in each other's homes or went on holiday together. The relationship proved a lifesaver during later years when I was working full-time but I am still conscious that we might look like a bit of an exclusive club to a newcomer moving to the street. Those first introductions need to work both ways, even though it may seem a bit artificial to knock on the door and introduce yourself, or to charge up to someone else in the sandpit of the local playground it is worth taking a deep breath and doing it.

There is also now a range of online sites like mumsnet.com and netmums.com that don't just offer the chance to take part in national debates via blogs and chatrooms but also drill down into what is available at a local level in every area, which can lead to opportunities to meet other like-minded local parents. A recent search, checking out my own neighbourhood using one of these sites, took me directly to the one o'clock club where I had spent so many happy hours when my children were small – but which had taken me at least a year to find twenty years ago.

Some friendships will last and others won't. When I gave up full-time work the first time round it was initially just a relief to spend at least part of my week getting to know other new mothers, at the swings and various other local meeting points which drew in families from all backgrounds and all ages. Over time I gradually worked out the ones I had most in common with, and they were usually like me, working in an ad hoc fashion while their children were young because they also wanted to spend time with them.

Friendships with some of the mothers who didn't work fizzled out. I gradually got bored with hearing about how many teeth, words and skills their children had and began to wonder whether some mothers had transferred the competitive edge they may have used to good effect in the workplace to their children, as the number of teeth escalated into a seemingly endless round of school runs and travelling to extracurricular music, drama, gymnastic and French lessons which replaced their daily commute. I daresay they got fed up with my unreliability as my freelance career ebbed and flowed.

When my older children started at their local nursery and primary school and I was offered a flexible contract as a feature writer on a daily paper, it was in some ways a relief to escape the constraints of a fairly solitary life working at home and the limited social horizons of the swings. But a little bird inside me was always nagging away about what I might be missing, urging me not to lose touch completely, so I stood for the governing body of the children's school and joined the PTA. Even though I had, at a stroke, managed to create at least two other part-time jobs for myself which over the next ten years often entailed rushing between work and school in the middle of the day, I have never regretted it.

Those extra responsibilities gave me a reach beyond the school gate even when I couldn't be there in person and friendships forged in that time have stayed with us as the children have grown into young adults. The willingness of those, mostly women, to step in during a crisis, and to use their networks to keep an eye on the children once they started to get older and more independent, has proved invaluable.

For a while I couldn't even bring myself to admit to others that my third pregnancy, after a four-year gap, was yearned for because part of me missed the swings, the one o'clock club and the altogether slower, more grounded, pace of life that being at home with small children brings.

In fact, I then spent precious little time at either as I was back at work within a year of my daughter's birth, this time in national politics working with my partner Alastair for the then leader of the Opposition, Tony Blair, a career move that at times seemed removed from any sort of reality let alone the run-of-the-mill predictability of neighbourhood life.

However, if I hadn't taken a leap into the dark and given up my full-time job in my first year of maternity, I would probably never have known what I was missing. Weighing up the costs of having thrown in my full-time career against the benefits of having at least a foothold in that other world, tedious as the conversations about whether your child sleeps through the night, is potty trained, can read or ride a bike without stabilisers may be, I wouldn't have had it any other way.

Returning to work shouldn't mean sacrificing time with your children or the wider community, whether it is the school, the church, sporting activities or simply hanging out with friends, family and neighbours. As children grow older, they become more important, not less.

CHAPTER 5

The School Gates

The writer Caroline Corby, reflecting on the reasons why she gave up her full-time job in the city to become a stay-at-home mum, nailed the tipping point for her decision on a taxi journey she took while on an out-of-town business trip that coincided with the last day of her daughters' school term. By the time she reached her destination she realised that she wasn't to get a single day off during their eight-week summer holiday.

'I couldn't pretend the job was fine for me or my family any longer. Subcontracting a baby's care to a professional nanny was easier than leaving them now they were getting older. Homework was getting trickier and I wanted to be there to help. I knew few of my children's friends and none of their parents. And then there was music practice and endless after-school activities, all of which I missed. As the taxi drew up outside the low-rise building my decision was made. I asked the bemused driver to return to the station, I got the next train back to London, rang my boss and told him I wasn't coming back … ever.'

Children grow up. It is hard to imagine what that means in those early years of adjusting to motherhood, especially if going back to work does feel like a treadmill of ferrying children to childminders, nurseries and keeping your head above water. But a new chapter does open up once they are out of nappies. With a bit of luck they become more companionable and certainly more portable, as they don't need to be transported with mountains of baby paraphernalia.

Some mothers, looking back from the vantage point of being the parent of a teenager, see the interlude between the ages of four and ten as a golden, prolonged honeymoon. Even though it may not always seem like it at the time, it is an age when children have some independence, are easier to entertain and communicate with but are still within the parental sphere of control, that ill-defined and highly personal space which can become such a battleground when the burgeoning independence of their adolescent years may appear to turn them into much-loved strangers.

For working parents, though, the golden era can bring new challenges, especially once children start nursery or primary school. The costly day-long childcare needed for a new baby or a toddler may not be necessary any more, but what is the alternative?

Not being a physical presence at the school gate can also lead to a sense of loss and exclusion from the new social circle of mothers and children that is being formed. How do you get to know your children's friends or their parents if you're not in the playground mafia or your children are with a childminder or after-school club, making it difficult for them to socialise with other children, or for parents who are working to reciprocate if they do?

The flip side is the realisation that can gradually dawn on women who have scaled back their hours to be at home with little children, or who have stopped work completely; that not having a child at home during the day can mean a lot of empty, often boring, hours to fill after the packed lunches and beds have been made. Contemplating the search for a new job or even a new direction can be as challenging (and demoralising) as the momentous deci-sion to quit, especially if it involves facing up to the childcare choices for the first time.

Once she had quit her job, Caroline Corby quickly realised how much she missed bits of it, noticing that in a world without work there were 'fewer landmarks and one day merged into another'.

Writing in *The Times* she observed: 'After I dropped my chil-dren at school, empty days loomed ahead and I was bored and I discovered I wasn't alone because playground mums are also divided into two categories – the contents and the waverers.'

Realising eventually that she was a waverer, someone who couldn't resist the lure of work, she started writing children's books from home, regaining the deadlines and the discipline she craved, but with the flexibility she needed. Around 70 per cent of working-age women with children between the ages of five and ten are working but it is not unusual for careers and job to evolve to meet the changing lives of growing children and availability of childcare, especially as so much is now expected of parents when it comes to supporting their children's education.

The feeling that you should be trying harder to understand what your children are learning in school, staying in touch with teachers and overseeing homework can weigh heavily after a long day at work. Then there is the purely logistical task of managing after-school activities, organising an alternative timetable of events for the holidays and coping with the emotional turmoil that children's ever changing friendship groups can bring when they sometimes spill over into accusations of bullying, causing huge unhappiness.

All three- and four-year-olds are now entitled to 12.5 hours a week of free early learning and this can take place in a state or private nursery, preschool playgroup or with a childminder. There aren't many jobs that can be done in this time. I well remember the elation of realising my last child was finally going to nursery only to realise that once I had dropped off, spent time settling her in and got home, there was just about time for a cup of coffee before she needed picking up again. Even with a full-time nursery school place between 9 and 3.30, extra childcare hours from somewhere may be necessary.

Although nearly all preschool children are now in some form of early education there are huge regional differences in where they take up that entitlement. In some parts of the country the majority of all preschool children use their 12.5 hours a week in state nursery schools or nursery classes attached to schools. In others, the majority of children are in private or voluntary sector nurseries or day-care centres until they are rising five and approaching compulsory education.

For parents who are already working with full-time day care in place, the offer of a part- or full-time place in a nursery class linked to a primary school, as opposed to a day nursery, may be impossible to organise once their child turns three if it can't be coordinated with other childcare arrangements.

For mothers like Julia, keeping her son in the private day nursery he had been attending since he was a baby, even though it had been failed by Ofsted, felt like the only option. It saved her money, as he still took up his 2.5 free hours of education in his day nursery but she did not have to find someone to take him out of the nursery to a school-based nursery class, then bring him back in the middle of the day. She felt that, since he would be moving to primary school within a year anyway, expecting him to settle in two different places for such a short period would be unnecessarily difficult and disruptive.

But keeping children in a day nursery that isn't linked to a school can have consequences. Rachel, a hospital consultant, made a similar decision, to keep her eldest child Amy in a private nursery when she was also entitled to take up a place in a school-based nursery, because it was the only way she could manage the complicated four-day week shift system she worked. Rachel had previously opted for a nursery because she actively preferred the idea of children being in group care to them being alone at home with a nanny.

'When Amy turned three she got her two-and-a-half hours a day of nursery schooling in the same place with the most fantastic teacher so I was very happy about that.

'But there was an enormous problem when she started school because 80 per cent of the children already knew each other from the nursery and I knew very few of the mums.

'We had felt we couldn't send her to the school nursery earlier because who was going to pick her up after two-and-a-half hours? It was only later that I realised so many of the children locally would have been at the school nursery but, anyway, that's the way it was. It did mean she hated school at the start because she had no friends and just didn't want to go at all. It's got much better over time and she's got friends now, but I am very aware of the fact that other mothers invite children over to their houses for tea and she started to read things into that because she knew she wasn't being invited anywhere. But that may also be because she is in the after-school club four days a week too.'

Her daughter's unhappiness persuaded Rachel that some change in her working hours was inevitable. She rearranged her hours to give herself one free afternoon to pick up her daughter, meet other mums, arrange 'playdates' and either take her to after-school activities or meet the teacher if necessary, although as a self-confessed workaholic who adores her job, she admits that was difficult.

'I guess the bottom line is, I've never been very good with socialising with people, I've never had a great network of friends and even if I stayed at home full-time I don't think that would change. I think that's my personality, so getting to know other mums in this area is a problem for me but I can now see that I might want to work less as they get older.'

Being freed of the financial commitments of full-time childcare can be liberating. Jane hung on to her job as a feature writer on the regional newspaper that effectively demoted her once she got pregnant, then soldiered on through her children's early years, putting up with the negativity of colleagues and their sexist comments because she and her husband needed the money to keep up their heavy mortgage payments. It was only when her children were both finally in primary school that she felt she could walk away from a difficult, hostile working environment and take a risk on a new career.

Sipping tea in the large sunny kitchen of the stylish detached house she and her husband have now finished renovating, she explains: 'There was no way I could afford to stop work altogether but I was offered the chance to go and work for a PR company run by a friend of mine. She'd got a child of her own so I felt I was in a position to stipulate which days I wanted to work and what time I wanted to leave in the evenings so that I could get back for the after-school club.

'The children's needs always came first although in many ways I was having a fantastic time too. The children were happy at school and on the days when I wasn't working, I was going to the gym, having a spot of lunch, going to the supermarket and just being a mum and I really enjoyed that.'

The right to ask for flexible work should in theory be particularly helpful to mothers of school-age children, especially once it is extended to parents of children up to the age of sixteen. Employers are still not obliged to agree to the request and have a number of 'permitted grounds' they can use to turn it down. However, some research has found that many women are still not aware they are eligible to request a different sort of working day if they have been in their jobs for six months.

Nevertheless, a supportive employer can help working parents to find imaginative ways of being more flexible to meet their family's needs, not necessarily simply going part-time. Other alternatives include varying hours around a 'core' time, banking hours over a longer period – which can help with the school holidays – or even job-sharing with a colleague or working term-time only and taking unpaid leave in the holidays.

In Jane's case, even working in a more sympathetic, family-friendly environment still didn't bring her the flexibility she needed especially when her boss, also a working mother, tried to change the days she worked. She gradually realised that her chances of promotion were also limited, so she decided to start up her own company instead.

'I wanted to work everything around the children and walk them to school every day. Everything just felt such a rush having to drop them off so I could be at my desk working for someone else at nine o'clock. Now I am able to walk to school every day, I pick them up two days a week and they go to the after-school club on the other three days. I'm very particular that when they come home I give them my time and attention and then, as soon as they go to bed, the computer goes back on and it could be midnight before I finish.'

Starting a business which can be run from home is often the fantasy dream for women tied to an unfriendly office, a long commute or trying to find ways to get back into work after a career break but being self-employed at home isn't always simple. Even though the business has now quadrupled in size, has a loyal group of clients, five employees and several freelance members of staff, and a small office close to both Jane's home and her children's school, she initially found working from home required self-discipline and motivation which was hard to summon without the structure of office routine around her.

'I used to put on my velour tracksuit to take the kids to school and then not actually get out of it all day. Then people would ask me for a coffee or I would just be sitting and working at home and think I'll just get the chicken out for tea or put some washing on, so it was too distracting. Getting an office was essential but I have kept everything very local and I do still have to rely on friends and fellow working mums when it gets a bit hairy or when I am travelling, because my husband works very long hours and I can't rely on him at all.'

Good after-school and holiday provision in her area played a vital part in helping Jane create a more flexible work-life balance. The National Childcare Strategy isn't just about nursery care; it also promises to put round-the-clock childcare for children up to the age of fourteen in every community by the end of the decade. That should encompass breakfast clubs and after-school clubs, which parents can mix and match to their needs.

The same Ofsted-rated standards which apply to day nurseries and childminders apply to all these types of out-of-school care for older children, whether it is an extended day offered by a local primary school or a kids' club or holiday play centre. These may be run by the voluntary sector, a local authority or private provider and are often based in sports centres, church or community centres or parks as well as schools.

The quality of care and the relationships between adults and children are no less important as they get older and anyone looking at after-school clubs should check that it provides that same safe, nurturing environment in which older children can chill out a bit, do their homework and take part in other structured activities.

Extended schools in particular are supposed to offer music tuition, sport and other extra-curricular activities. However, provision is still a bit patchy and costs do vary – the average cost of an after-school club varies from £35 to £45 for fifteen hours a week in England and summer play schemes average around £87 a week across the UK, although some can soar to over £2,000 for the long six-week summer holiday if parents pay additional costs for meals, trips and days out.

Provision of after-school care and breakfast clubs is also variable and many parents still report that they can't access enough affordable care – and particularly enough holiday childcare places – for older or disabled children. However, the Daycare Trust's Listening to Children survey suggests that when after-school care and holiday play schemes are available they are popular. Older children particularly value being able to spend time with their friends trying out new activities that they might not otherwise have a chance to do rather than being on their own at home, where they might just end up stuck in front of the TV or playing computer games.

Good after-school clubs also provide a stepping stone to the independence that the later teenage years offer, although some of the young people interviewed also talked about their preference for young, active staff. They did voice fears about having to walk home alone in the dark once the club had closed, but also acknowledged that after-school clubs and holiday schemes were good for their parents because it helped them go to work in the knowledge that their children were safe and well looked after.

But just as day nurseries aren't everyone's preferred option, after-school clubs don't suit every family. Caitlin's decision to work full-time while her first daughter was tiny, so that her husband didn't bear the full financial weight of supporting the family, meant relying on a combination of a childminder, her mother and her husband, who worked from home so could fit in odd hours of childcare where necessary.

However, she admits that after the birth of her second child and as the transition to nursery school loomed for her elder daughter, she found herself reassessing her priorities. She saw a reflection of herself in younger female colleagues who were still working long, punishing hours and then worrying that they didn't have time for a social life or couldn't meet a boyfriend.

'I felt like saying to them, "Look, get a life, you can knock out the last 20 per cent of what you are doing, no one's going to realise it's not happening, it's only you who wants it done." I also found myself weighing up what really mattered – and work never seemed to be quite as important as it used to be.'

Reassessing her priorities as the children got older brought changes in her job and her childcare arrangements in its wake. 'When they are little they are not doing anything are they? But I found it got more pressurised as they got older. By the time I was on maternity leave with my second, I had a one-and-a-half-year-old and I had started to go to mother and toddler groups. I'd met a really good network of friends who all lived up and down my road, so the community thing started to kick in and I didn't want to give that up completely because I thought, this is an opportunity, I have got new friends who live around me, they all have children and a lot had daughters who were the same age as mine and we all really got on together.

'Then they started going to nursery and the next thing there was the sports day to go to, the Mother's Day Tea to attend, then they were at school and suddenly there were all these other things I wanted to do and events I wanted to be at. I think you just want to meet the other mums, you want to know what your child's social life has become because if you are at work all the time you don't really know.'

Having negotiated a four-day week with her employers she still found life was almost harder than it had been when she worked full-time with a small baby, partly because the childcare that had worked well for two preschool-age children suddenly seemed inadequate.

'The start of primary school was one of the most stressful periods in my life. I had to get the children to the childminder by a certain time so that my daughter could get a lift to school and so my whole very easy routine had to change all of a sudden. She was quite happy at school, it was just the change of routine that *I* found stressful to deal with. Sometimes I would get her to the childminder on time but the lift wouldn't be there and I'd end up taking her to school, and the childminder's house wasn't very big so it just suddenly didn't seem to work very well.'

Even when the children had outgrown the childminder, the prospect of an after-school club didn't appeal to Caitlin: 'I realised that I wanted the girls to be able to do all the things after school that I'd been able to do, like ballet lessons, or going to Brownies. Childminders often look after too many children and they can't shove them all in a car just to take one to ballet.

'So I decided really that my only route was a nanny at that point, which was really stupid in some ways because I ended up paying her a full-time wage and spending more on my childcare than I did when they weren't at school. But she did the cleaning, my ironing, my washing and the school holiday cover, plus she had her own baby, who was three months old, and she stayed until he started school and became part of my family. She was a good disciplinarian and had similar values to us, which was great, and she has remained a firm family friend. The children still go to sleepovers at her house.

'Oddly enough, it was as the children got older that I started to realise how incredibly important the quality of childcare is. I have always said to my husband that I was happy to work to support him but I never ever wanted to have to worry about childcare even if it meant paying over the odds for it.

'If we hadn't found a nanny, we would have had to reconsider our options,' says Caitlin. 'And I would probably have worked three days a week but I didn't really want to do that because the balance would have shifted from being at work more than at home to being at home more. I think I would have felt compromised about my role. The other benefits are that I don't have to rush home from work and look after my children, which is a trap I think some women fall into once they start to work more flexible hours.'

Employing someone full-time just at the moment that you actually need fewer hours of care may seem perverse but many women, and I was one of them, fall into the trap of thinking that because their children are at school, looking after them isn't an issue any more and can be squeezed in easily around work or using a mix of after-school care and flexible working. Rushing to get home from work before the end of the school day or before the play centre closes and getting there in a flap can diminish the imagined satisfaction of picking up your own children, especially if it has to be mixed up with other household chores.

'By the time I get home the children have been looked after, they have had their tea, and I don't have to rush them around to piano lessons or ballet,' says Caitlin. 'That's all happened whilst I've been at work. I can fit my shopping in at lunchtime so I feel luckier than a lot of other people who may be squeezing their hours at work, not taking a break, and then trying to do everything else in the evening.

'I have got friends who do that and they say they are always knackered because they are rushing around doing all the other things after work. And when other mums who are thinking of going back ask me how I do it, I always say get a cleaner and someone else to do all those things and everybody will think you run a wonderful home.'

The new arrangement was so successful that Caitlin eventually went back to work full-time again when her youngest daughter started primary school. But there was a cost: 'I actually regret that because I never really got to know the mums in her class very well. A lot of them didn't work or they worked part-time and they did a lot of the picking up from school and dropping off in the morning.

'It's very difficult when you get the letter asking if you can come and help with the reading or another activity that takes place during the school day – the children would like me to be there.'

There will inevitably be guilty feelings about letting children down. I can remember doing a two-hour round trip quite regularly from central to north London, where my children were at primary school, to watch a fifteen-minute class assembly which the school insisted on doing at two in the afternoon for some reason. Once I had done it for one child, I had to do it for all three so it became a fairly regular trek. The time had to be made up by working later, but it was worth it to see the sheer pleasure on their faces. They do now talk about how much they looked forward to the days when one of us could pick them up from school, even though they had nannies they loved, but we will never know how much that was only because it had novelty value for quite a long time and seemed like a bit of a treat.

Some school-based events and activities are easier to fit around work than others. Getting to the Summer Fair at the weekend or sneaking out of work for annual events like the Nativity show or the

Christmas party are usually manageable and offer at least a brief glimpse of other parents and, possibly, the teachers.

But the expectation that parents will play an 'active' part in their children's education has never been higher than it is today and can lead to more inner conflict. For parents whose only real experience of the education system is their own school days – when parental involvement meant one parents' meeting, one yearly report and two sets of public exams, and subjects like maths were taught in an entirely different way – the pressure to make the right school choice and keep up with the cycle of SATS, league tables and public exams can be both baffling and wearing.

That piece of homework or letter from the school, found late at night because you have only just got round to checking the book bag or the planner, or not found at all until it is too late, can feel like a sharp reproach that you are not being a good enough mother, communicating well enough with teachers or keeping a beady enough eye on your children's progress.

According to one government report, the amount of time parents spend doing homework or reading with their children has increased fourfold in the last thirty years. Overall, that is a good thing. There is plenty of evidence to show that when parents are actively engaged, encouraging and supportive, their children do better at school.

But the term 'parental involvement' has now become a catch-all expression which can cover everything from becoming a governor, organising school events, joining the PTA, exercising 'rights' and campaigning for better and different provision as well as staying on top of your own child's progress, homework, spelling, after-school activities and evening reading sessions.

A cursory look at the volume of educational books and revision guides in most of the big bookshops bears witness to how rapidly the market for pressured parents is growing. Even parents who can be in the playground at the end of the school day feel the strain, but for those juggling work and more than one child it feels almost like another part-time job. It is then terrifyingly easy to get caught up in the herd anxiety about your children 'falling behind', to feel that you also need to be teaching them at home and assume that every other non-working parent is managing to support their children's schoolwork better, calmly and more methodically, and without the blistering, futile and often counterproductive rows that can erupt when tired children and stressed parents collide too late in the evening.

They are probably not; letters from school and homework have a mysterious way of eluding even the most dogged, hands-on parents. All school performance tables now show the 'value added' that the school provides and the chances are that if your children are in a school that is good enough, and there is a mass of information out there to show whether or not it is, there is no reason why he or she shouldn't be doing well without excessive intervention at home unless they have particular special needs.

Nancy, a lone parent who struggled with a traumatic relationship breakdown with her husband when her daughter was a baby, was forced to put her into a school some distance from home as it was the only one in the area that had the after-school club she needed to keep working. A flexible working system allowed her to continue full-time but collect her daughter one afternoon a week. But she still needed to take extra time off to meet the teachers who were supporting her daughter's special needs.

'I found it very hard when they told me she was behind for her age. But I have worked with the school and we have a programme of homework and spellings that I have to help her with every night which means coming home from work and religiously sitting with her while she practises her reading and writing.

'Sometimes I end up in the kitchen cooking and shouting the words to her and there have been moments when it has been very hard. Because her reading levels were low, the school was sending home words that she couldn't even pronounce so it does take time and I sometimes feel it is too much pressure for her and me. I don't think I can expect her to go to the after-school club every night so I can go to work and then come home and do even more work.'

Parents like Nancy who are working and can't always be there at the end of the day do need to be able to hear quickly from their children's teachers if things are going wrong, and also to be able to communicate their concerns and anxieties to the school. Nancy says she has never found communicating with the school hard. 'I fix the meetings with the special needs teacher then I go to my line manager, who has always been really sympathetic and has always let me take time off to go to the school. They do ring me if they need to and I can always ring them. I would never ring up about an issue, though, unless Iona was really unhappy, which hasn't happened yet.'

Letters and phone calls are quite old-fashioned in today's world. Websites and email communication are much more efficient tools with which to communicate between home and school, not just for personal concerns but to find out which topics your children will be covering in each term. As they get older you should ideally also be able to find on the school website which exam board they are taking, what is in the syllabus, what the school is offering in the curriculum for each different subject and, if possible, to see a timetable for coursework exams and modules. If your child's class teacher or form tutor or head teacher can't offer this, or the school doesn't have a website that is kept up to date, maybe you should ask the school why.

There is still a huge question mark over how much parents actually need to be involved in the daily life of their children's school. Much of the evidence about parental involvement in education suggests there may be strong social and emotional reasons for being known in the playground, it is what goes on at home that really matters.

The research reviews carried out by Professor Charles Desforges concluded that 'at home parenting' was around six times more important than the 'school effect' on how primary-age children perform. Rather than rushing home from work to practise SATs papers with their children or worrying that they aren't in daily contact with their children's teachers, parents could have as much of an impact on their children's success at school by developing a 'parenting style' which is typified by warmth, good communication, aspiration, confidence and suitable boundaries.

Simply talking to them about what they have learned at school, what they have enjoyed and what has not gone so well may be just as valuable as forcing them into extra work that is better suited to the classroom when what they really want to do is unwind in their own time. When I heard Professor Desforges lecture on this subject several years ago, he was specifically asked by a member of the audience whether there was any evidence to suggest that working parents were responsible for their children performing less well at school. His answer: 'none at all'.

Mothers don't need to feel they are disadvantaging their children by working but there is a tricky balance to be struck by all parents whether they are working or not. Finding the happy medium between paying attention to children's school lives, engaging with their other interests and keeping consistently high expectations without panicking, resorting to draconian punishments, head-on confrontations or – even worse – doing homework or coursework for them, is difficult, especially if the whole process has to be fitted into a couple of hours in the evening when there are other children to attend to, bath and feed.

And while not panicking is an art to perfect, avoiding the temptation just to give up is equally important. Most research now shows that the children who do least well at school, regardless of their social, class or cultural backgrounds, are the ones whose parents, whether working or not, don't take an interest in them at all.

CHAPTER 6

Latchkey Teens

Working part-time as a family lawyer when her children were small and at primary school suited Liz well. She loved the stimulation she got from her work as much as being able to go to the mother and toddler group. Her childcare fell into place quickly when the family cleaner, who lived in the same village in south Wales, offered to look after her first baby when she went back to work.

'She was about twenty years older than I was, her kids were grown up and she was very keen to have grandchildren herself. She was just one of those women who are fantastic with babies. I'd go out in the morning and she'd be doing the jigsaw with John and I'd come back in the evening and she'd be doing it for the eighteenth time which was great, because I'm not actually brilliant with puzzles and singing the nursery rhymes and all that stuff. We loved her to bits, she became godmother to my second child, but her strength was definitely small children and she was fine to do the pick-ups and school holidays when they were little and took the whole going to school thing in her stride.'

As her son started secondary school she thought she had got her work-life balance perfectly sorted out: 'I thought we were moving into that classic time when conventionally you are supposed to get your career in gear again because the children are becoming more independent.'

Nothing could have been further from the truth. Within three years she was at home full-time, having thrown in her career for a life pottering around her kitchen and doing a bit of volunteering at the Citizens Advice Bureau. The realisation that the golden era of primary school can give way to a tumultuous ten years of prepubescent moods, unanswered mobile phones and public exams started slowly.

'As they got older they started to want to do things that our carer couldn't always accommodate because she didn't drive. In the school holidays her idea was still that they would always be in our house or her house. But my son would have other ideas – he would want to go and play football on the other side of town or meet up with his mates and I started to feel bad about that.'

Accepting that the arrangement had run its course was difficult but Liz, an ebullient, talkative and determined feminist, was adamant that she would keep working. The children went to an after-school club but even then her son wasn't really happy because he always wanted to be out and about doing things with his friends. She tried to work more regimented hours, within the discipline of court appearances and client meetings, so she could always be there if they needed picking up, until one January morning in the year her eldest started secondary school.

'I just had this epiphany in a week when both kids were ill and had spent two nights with their heads in a bucket and both of us were either in court in the morning or in client meetings all day. The second time it happened within a week my husband just said, "Do you fancy stopping work?" I thought about it for a bit, because I had to give three months' notice, but then handed in my notice within about forty-eight hours. My employers were baffled.'

Looking back now, with her children aged fifteen and seventeen, and settled into a part-time job at the CAB that grew out of her volunteering, Liz has few regrets that she was at home full-time during the children's teenage years.

'It was just like this cloud lifting because even though I had a lot of free time when they were healthy and fit and everything was going well at school, there was also slack so, if someone did call from school and say one of them had a splinter in their eye, I could just go, sort it out.

'I did end up doing the eighteen-mile round trip to school three or four times a week. The school is nine miles from where we live, so if you miss the afternoon bus there is no way of getting home and when my son was doing his GCSEs he discovered this work ethic, which surprised us hugely, but meant he wanted to stay at school until five o'clock.

'I didn't have to worry about leaving a child alone at home if they were ill or worry about the gradual independence they wanted to have. I don't know anybody, apart from my parents or possibly a close relative, who could really monitor the movements of a teenager when they tell you they are going down to the park after school, which may be appropriate at their age until you realise they don't have their mobile switched on or become vague about the time they will be back.

'I was always able to keep an eye on my watch and I knew I

could be down there quickly if there was a problem. Our only other route would have been to get an au pair, we've got the space, but I don't know whether a perfectly nice eighteen, nineteen-year-old without much English would have the authority and be quite street-wise enough, to deal with all that.'

The crucial years between thirteen and eighteen can provide a second tipping point for working mothers, especially if they don't have family nearby to step in. Moving to secondary school can bring a host of new issues to contend with, as children move from the safety of a small school with one main class teacher to a far bigger, different environment with up to ten or twelve new teachers for pupils and parents to get to know, (all of whom may have different preferred methods of communicating with their students' homes). Parents can no longer hang around at the gate at the end of the day. Even if they have the flexibility at work to do that, many teenagers consider it the equivalent of a social death.

A surge of brain growth in early adolescence, linked to the ability to control emotions and make rational judgements, is now thought to be similar in magnitude to the one which takes place in the toddler years. But toddlers do usually wear themselves out by a reasonable time in the evening, don't vanish for hours on end with their friends, spend hours on the phone or plugged into a set of earphones and lose themselves in social networking sites over which parents have no control.

The struggle with a recalcitrant toddler or screaming baby can pale into insignificance compared to the sometimes venomous anger and loathing that can ensue from rows about homework and revision in an era when parents feel they, too, are being judged and found wanting if their children don't achieve; or the sheer panic when you are at work and realise a child hasn't arrived home from school and no one knows where they are.

The demands made by teenagers can be momentous, frustrating and occasionally lead parents to feel they are losing control at home and at work as children who have previously been loving and communicative start to assert their independence and become argumentative, unpredictable and self-obsessed.

Writer Kate Figes, in her book *The Terrible Teens*, believes society hasn't yet worked out that it needs to allow parents extra leeway to cope with adolescents in the way we forgive the need to deal with smaller children.

'For the best part of a decade adolescents learn how to master the mental skills essential to survive on their own and it is often a tortuous process,' she says. 'All too often, adult society misses opportunities to educate and guide adolescents when their intellectual skills are at their most malleable. When children are small we patiently teach them how to read and write, how to count or tie their shoelaces because we know that these are essential skills. Yet when our children reach adolescence, we often withdraw and offer less guidance because they are so much more capable physically of doing things for themselves.'

If society generally doesn't offer much support, understanding or compassion to the parents of teenagers, in the world of work they are virtually invisible. Employers can't easily avoid more family-friendly legislation on maternity leave or the right to ask for flexible work, and it might now be more acceptable to phone the office and say the baby is sick, but as Liz says with almost twenty years of experience behind her: 'For working parents, it is the things that come out of the blue like the phone calls from school, whether about coursework or a disciplinary issue, or the day you don't know where they are.

'Taking time off because you need to find a time to talk to your teenager when they want to talk to you, or sort out a school issue, is still taboo in most workplaces. I shudder to think what would have happened if I had still been at work on the day I got an urgent call from my son's school, at 4.30pm, to say his coursework had been called in for moderation and could we present it at school by five o'clock. Even now I feel sure that it was only my maternal instinct that led me to find it in the bin with five minutes to spare, but interrupting or cancelling an important meeting to rush home and look for it would have been unthinkable.'

Psychotherapist Rozsika Parker in her book about motherhood *Torn in Two* claims the pressure on children to achieve at school can lock parents and adolescents in a war of attrition at the worst possible moment for both. 'Finding a sense of themselves which is distinct from their parents and their childhood selves is one of the central developmental tasks of the age group,' she says. 'The tools employed include opposition, evasion and a necessary questioning of all their parents stand for.

'Entry into puberty and secondary education represents a protracted crisis of separation. Often it involves a kind of mourning – for lost childhood and lost certainties. Parents feel torn too, wanting their children to grow up so that they can move to a new stage of their parenthood yet mourning the fact that the very qualifications they long for their child to obtain successfully will open the door to their departure. With mounting ambivalence they have to bear the strain of children fighting for independence, battling for freedom, yet all the while maintaining a reproachful dependence.'

The conflict between independence and that reproachful dependence means there is no such thing as ideal childcare for a teenager, especially if they have strong ideas about how they want to be spending their time and are too old for the after-school club, too young to be left alone completely and are unwilling to accept limits on their freedom from their parents, let alone an au pair or nanny.

Giving up work altogether is not a realistic option. Almost 80 per cent of working-age women whose youngest child is between eleven and fifteen are in some sort of employment. If they work for themselves, like Jane after she set up her own PR business, the working day can be more pliable.

'My daughter is about to start at a secondary school where they are trialling "continental hours" which means they will start at eight and finish at two. This has sent me into a bit of a tailspin because I don't really want her to be a latchkey kid so I will have to change my business to accommodate that and give more responsibility to the people that are working for me, which is hard because I am a bit of a control freak,' she explains.

But in different circumstances the temptation to give them a key and let them fend for themselves in the late afternoon, and even in the holidays, can be overwhelming. Gill is a slim pale brunette and a lone parent in her early thirties whose spacious top-floor flat is only a ten-minute walk from her sixteen-year-old daughter's South London secondary school. She felt that the child was old enough to cope with coming home alone in the early years of secondary school while Gill was retraining as a solicitor. Cash was in short supply and there was no obvious carer to be found locally, although a neighbour's family had said their house would always be open to Lauren after school if she was alone.

But Gill found out the hard way that simply leaving young teenagers to their own devices until you come home from work can be high risk. 'I always knew there would be worrying times while I was at work. Even if they have their mobile phone and they may say they are at a friend's house, how would you ever know if they're not? I did try and keep all the lines of communication open and not to be too strict because I wanted her to feel she could tell me anything without any repercussions and have no need to rebel.

'But there was a time she had a friend round and they were in the living room and her friend was jumping around a bit, and she put her hand on the window to get on to the chair and a great big part of the glass came out.

'She could have severed an artery she bled so badly, but I was at work at the time and had my phone switched off. I eventually got this message so I dashed home by which time everything had been dealt with by my neighbours.

'Kids had been playing out on the street and luckily no one was hurt but you can imagine a piece of glass as big as a dinner plate had gone down and smashed into a million pieces. If a kid had been down there it would have been really dangerous. I had to ban children from the house and she would either have to go round to their houses after school if she wanted to see them or she had to go to a neighbour or an after-school club so she had that time filled before I came home from work.'

Who's to judge whether Gill was right or wrong? Every one of us will have been in that situation with older children at some time. Things can go wrong even if older children are being 'looked after'. I once left my sixteen-year-old son allegedly looking after his younger sister and her friend, only to come home and find them in a kitchen full of smoke. The girls had tried to cook something in foil in the microwave while he was plugged into his computer upstairs, blissfully oblivious to the chaos going on ten feet below him.

Some young people may be better able to cope with being left home alone than others, especially if there is a neighbour nearby to touch base with in case of emergencies, food that doesn't need cooking and regular phone contact with Mum and Dad. Parents whose children come to any harm while being left home alone under sixteen could, technically, be prosecuted for neglect. But even if there were suitable after-school arrangements locally – and some official estimates suggest that there are only twenty thousand childcare places for the four million eleven to fourteen-year-olds in this country – they often appear unappealing to young adolescents.

Over time the trust between Gill and her daughter was gradually rebuilt and Lauren started to go home alone again. She has a different take on being a latchkey kid: 'I never felt lonely or scared. To be honest as soon as I was able to use a key to get in, I thought I would be fine on my own.

'I just used to make myself something to eat and watch TV and I didn't really do many silly things. Some of my friends would be so excited when their parents weren't there and say, "Wow, come over I have a free house," but I had a free house all the time, so it didn't seem that special to sort of break the rules.'

Now studying for A levels, Lauren says she is stunned by how dependent are some of her friends with non-working parents. 'They still go with their parents to do things like the doctor, the dentist or the bank whereas I have been doing all that on my own for a couple of years and as the trust between Mum and me has grown I have got better at calling her all the time to tell her where I am!'

If you have teenagers and younger children a nanny share may still work as the older children can justify it to their friends on the grounds they are technically caring for a younger sibling, but finding someone who wants to take on the hassle of looking after a couple of teenagers can be hard; many nannies really prefer babies. Another option may be to advertise for classroom assistants in local schools who want to earn a bit of extra money. They are inevitably CRB-checked, have some knowledge of children and education and may come with references from the head teacher. They are also likely to be on term-time contracts, and therefore free in the holidays. Some are young men, which is helpful if you have teenage boys. Even if they are not actually doing much work, it is cheaper than paying someone full-time, but still provides someone in the background until you get home from work.

It is quite possible that many of our children don't need as much of the attention that we feel obliged to give. In her book *Perfect Madness* the American writer Judith Warner claims that modern post-baby boomer mothers have used liberation to become 'a generation of perfectionist control freaks, more concerned with creating the perfect playgroup or tracking down the last gram of trans fat in their kids' crackers than in running, or changing, or even participating in the larger world'.

That may be more true of the USA than the UK but even so, it is possible to lose perspective on how much children do need their parents while they are growing into adulthood. Work can bring some valuable distance between a truculent teenager and his or her frustrated parents and give adolescents some of the space they need to learn independence and self-reliance.

After my partner Alastair and I both quit our full-time jobs at the same time as our older children were approaching GCSEs, thinking they would be delighted at the prospect of our undivided attention, the mother of my younger son's best friend told me she overheard him complaining that he now had to come home from school every day and find his parents in the kitchen, when he really just wanted to be alone.

He has since told me that it might have helped him more if we hadn't been at home all the time. He felt we just created more stress by always wanting to know what he was doing, and how much he had been revising, questions that we would almost certainly have asked less frequently if we hadn't been working at home. He is convinced he would have done just as well without our input, though I am not so sure.

Part-time school teacher Anne says her love-hate relationship with her thirteen-year-old daughter means that one minute she wants her mum at home at the end of the day so she can make her something to eat and hear all the news, but the next minute she can be totally 'obnoxious'.

'She can be really awful sometimes. Everything is my fault, everything I say is wrong, even if it is the right thing it is wrong, I think she just wants to attack me personally because I am close to her. It can be hard to get the balance right and I am grateful for the days I don't get back until six, because she and her brother and sister are with their grandparents and I think it is quite good for me to be a step removed.'

John Coleman, who founded the Trust for the Study of Adolescence, believes there is no reason why a successful career can't co-exist with being the mother of a teenager because the critical element to any child-parent relationship is quality, not quantity. 'It's perfectly possible for you to work very, very hard or do long hours but still have a good relationship with your kids,' he says. 'What matters is what is in that relationship – trust, recognition, understanding and support.'

Above all parents must 'endorse' their teenagers' hobbies and activities by showing an interest. 'Even if you can't get to the football match or the school play, you need to care about the results and how it went or make sure your children have the right equipment which says "What is important to you is important to me too". We know that where parents show an interest and support or endorse what the young person is doing, that young person feels better, they have a better self-concept and they are much more likely to achieve and to want to do the best for themselves.'

At times though, it requires a huge effort of will and restraint to manage a warm and affectionate interest in a teenager who has just delivered his or her 'You're The Last Person I Want To Talk To' line, told you they hate you, or even worse, that they know you hate them. 'If you go in with your agenda and say I want to talk about this but you don't leave any room for their agenda, then communication will never be very effective,' says Dr Coleman. 'Much better to say, "I've got some things I want to discuss but I want to hear about what you're worrying about," then it can be magic really.'

Above all don't give up on them. The easy path for parents who are very busy, faced with the realisation that their children just aren't going to stay the same as they were in primary school, is to think 'we'll leave them to their own devices' rather than deal with the new, truculent behaviour. This is the worst possible reaction.

Much of the research into parenting 'styles' separates parents into four main categories: authoritarian, indulgent, indifferent and authoritative. Again and again the evidence suggests that parenting that is either too disciplinarian and unyielding or too laid-back and permissive works less well in the long run. Young people whose home life is warm and supportive and an environment in which good communication is balanced by an acceptance of burgeoning independence but some boundaries tend to do better in terms of self-esteem, achievement and avoiding risky behaviour.

According to psychiatrist Philip Graham, author of *The End of Adolescence*: 'In contrast to authoritarian parents, *authoritative* parents do listen and negotiate and are prepared to make reasonable compromises though they stick firmly to boundaries once they think they have gone as far as they can. They tend to give children more responsibility and, in return, expect and get more help in the house. Throughout childhood and teen years they change their rules and expectations as their children become more competent, mature and responsible.'

That may mean accepting a new wide, disparate group of friends that you find hard to get to know, especially if you are not around after school, and that group may suddenly seem to have become the surrogate family, in whom they confide and with whom they enjoy the sort of activities you used to relish together. Our daughter's constant refrain is that *everything* – shopping, the cinema, going on holiday – would be so much more fun if her friends were there.

But they still need to know their parents are there for them in the background, especially if they are let down or rejected by their friends or get into trouble. Staying engaged is the key, while developing strategies that allow them to develop their independence and interests without putting so tight a structure around them they reject it altogether. However impossible they may seem, and however busy you are at work, it is what John Coleman calls 'money in the bank'. 'Whenever there is a row or some difficulty they know that you are still engaged and you will have common interests to fall back on.'

Anna, now studying for her A levels at a sixth-form college in Somerset, agrees it is a difficult balance. Both her parents worked while she and her older brother Peter were at primary school, but her mother took a career break from her job as a manager in the NHS to be at home with her and Peter once they started secondary school, and is now working again part-time. Anna firmly believes that, overall, having two working parents has bene-fitted them.

'Of course up until the age of around 12, I might not have felt entirely comfortable on my own all day. I think it's rather sad if a child has become totally independent by a young age – your parents should still be caring for you, just not too much,' she says.

'But in your teens I think a balance needs to be found but it's helpful not to have parents around all the time.

'The advantages of having parents at home are pretty obvious, they're always there if you need help, always around to take you places, or pick you up, and the housework tends to be done. But the disadvantages are that if a parent is constantly around to do all of this, how can a child really gain independence?

'Thanks to Mum and Dad not always being here during school holidays, etc., I've had to cook for myself, clean up after myself, and take responsibility for what I need to do that day. I think that creates a trust between a child and parent, knowing that a child can be left on their own and not let it end up in tragedy.

'And having experienced both having a mother working and not working throughout my teens, I must say that I do prefer it while she's working. This might just be me, but I found it reassuring to know that my mother was actually doing something productive that she enjoyed – not that she wasn't busy before, but she seemed to enjoy work.'

Mulling over with my eldest son recently whether or not I had been a 'good enough' mother in those teenage years before I stopped work, I was surprised to hear how strongly he felt that his relationship with us in his teenage years was fairly irrelevant compared to what he described as 'the groundwork that will have been laid long before the teenage years creep up'.

He argued that the inherent characteristics of his relationship with us were conditional on what happened in the first seven years of his life when we were much more likely to spend time with him and after which they are hard to change.

'If you really know each other by then, then you can get through anything and your relationship with your parents when you are a teenager, whether you work or not, is fundamentally affected by those years at the beginning,' he says. 'I think in secondary school you need your parents just to guide you in the right direction sometimes but it is when you are at a very young age that you develop what kind of person you are going to be.'

Seeing that relationship with your children over a twenty-year period as the wedge, described by child and adolescent psychiatrist Sebastian Kraemer, can help. At the start it is just you and the baby wrapped up in each other, then the father comes in, followed by grandparents, siblings, other carers and then friends. It gets thinner and thinner until the relationship with the mother is just one part of a much wider circle of friends and family. However, that relationship with their mother is still the building block on which everything later on is constructed. If it is fragile, it can be hard to rebuild later on in adolescence but if sturdy, it does provide a strong foundation to withstand later pressures that work, and hormones, may bring.

The temptation to give up work does have its downside. Liz admits that even though walking out of her solicitor's firm may have lifted a weight off her shoulders, it also brought a different, even more personal, sense of regret that she may no longer be providing her children, and particularly her daughter, with a positive role model.

'Later that year my daughter wrote a really sweet little poem for a Mother's Day celebration at school all about how I had given up my career,' says Liz. 'But that was hard for me because I'm well aware that I'm meant to be some sort of go-ahead she-male role model for her.

'I have got all these O levels, A levels, a good degree and I've got a bright teenage girl to whom I would like to have been maybe a different sort of example. She has never known me doing nothing but when people ask her what her parents do, she can't say that her father's an intellectual property partner in a major legal firm and her mother's a judge, which I might have been. She has to say her mother's someone who goes down to the CAB twice a week in her jeans.

'Sometimes she will say things like, "Have you been sitting at home drinking coffee again, Mum?" and I will think how cross I would have been if someone had said that about me when I was young or stopped me going back to work when they were babies.

'I have found all that stuff difficult because I am aware that the labels do matter and when other friends have stopped work I have even found myself thinking, "Well, what are you now then –

a housewife?" I am always careful to continue to say to people who ask me what I do, "I'm a solicitor, and I'm not working at the moment." That way I know I've still got a label that means something to other people, even if it might matter in some ways less to me.

'I hope my daughter knows that I'd proved everything that I needed to prove, that I have also now had five years of trying to make the most of being as good a mother as I can be, of being able to take them and their friends to places and being the one that could say, yes of course you can have sleepovers in the holidays, doing things that I was really pleased to be able to do, and was better at it than I would have been giving them the time when they were babies.'

The conflict between wanting to be a good mother and a good role model may be harder to resolve after a long career break. Starting a new career had been at the back of Hannah's mind once her daughters started at secondary school. She had given up a full-time job in fashion retail when they were tiny and taken ten years out while they were growing up, also volunteering while they were at primary school. But as her two daughters grew up, her awareness of how they saw her grew along with her fear of moving on.

'The girls like the idea of me having a job, they like being able to tell their friends that their mum used to be in the fashion business and they wish they could say that now.

'I think it is terribly complicated and stressful because that sense that I should be a better role model to them is clashing with a different kind of responsibility. I don't feel I have to be there to pick them up. They get themselves to and from school but I do feel the burden of their social life, their aspirations and their belief that they are totally in control of their lives.

'The world out there is much more cut-throat and no job is for life, so I feel I have to push them about doing their homework. They certainly don't need me as much as they did but I think the problem is more with me feeling that I can't leave them completely alone even as teenagers because I wouldn't be in control of their lives.'

And not working, being aware of what she might be missing personally, can rankle: 'It is frustrating when they are all over the place, and I think I made this choice for you and now look what you are doing. It doesn't mean you get perfect children.'

But just as there is no such thing as the perfect mother, there is no such thing as the perfect child, just different individuals who grow up in different ways. The first child might sail through his or her teenage years without a hiccup, collecting exam certificates, keeping the same friends and including you in that group. Another can veer off in an entirely different direction to the extent that you think they will never return to normal.

Dee's four children span twenty years and a divorce and remarriage. She has managed to stay working throughout, starting out as a bus driver, then eventually retraining as a journalist, getting a job on a newspaper in south London and following her dream to publish her own magazine. Problems with her son started when he was at primary school, at the time of her divorce, and his behavioural problems led to him getting a statement of special education needs.

By the time he started secondary school Dee was very busy 'freelancing to survive', exhausted by the job and her three teenage children. Having fought to become a professional from a working-class African–Caribbean background meant a lot to her and she wasn't prepared to give it up, but always managed to stay involved in what they were doing. 'However tired I was, I always put my family first and was hands-on. I made it my business to know what was going on in school, what their general deadlines were, even if they didn't know themselves, and I always gave them that extra push if necessary. They knew I would never tolerate bad behaviour.

'However, things got rocky. I even remember being called at work and told my son had climbed out the window once, but he did settle down and he developed this attitude that effort brings success and I think I was, I am, a role model. My older daughter is now a dancer and I remember when she was at school they were asked who their heroes were and she said "my mum" and I was really chuffed by that. She still attributes the drive that she has in her dancing career to me.

'They have all got this drive about them but I think it is my son we are all most proud of because even though he sometimes tells me off and says things like, you know, you said you were going to do this and you didn't, this boy that couldn't read properly at eleven did manage to leave secondary with qualifications because of the effort he put in.'

John Coleman's career as a psychologist working with teenagers has given him years of experience to reflect on. 'I've seen so many kids go through a period which just seems as if it's the end of the world, the parents can't see that any good's going to come out of this, he or she is a total failure or waste of time. But you know, two years later they say he's not quite as bad as he was and an awful lot of kids do come through, it is part of human development and parents sticking with their kids is terribly important, whether they are working or not.

'So don't give up, stay in there and if they're angry and if they're resentful and if they're difficult, just remember it's not you they're angry about, its what's happening inside them. Don't take it personally, however hard it is to just listen. If you could just step back a bit and realise that the anger and that terrible behaviour, well, it's the turmoil and chaos inside.'

CHAPTER 7

Who Does the Laundry?

At some of my lowest moments, when the term work-life balance seems like a washed-out description of what feels more like work-life battle, I have often felt the dilemma of managing children, a job and a relationship came down to one simple question: 'Who takes out the black bin bags?' There are several other versions of it: 'Who does the laundry/Who irons the shirts?'

I was once tempted to quit my then job on the spot after I fell down the stairs (wearing stupid shoes) carrying a basket of laundry in between coming home from Downing Street and going out to a work-related dinner. However, the bulging black bag, usually the last thing left to do at night, usually trumps all else as a reminder of my mother's early warning to me when she retrained as a teacher in her forties that 'there was no such thing as women's lib, women simply do two jobs'.

The banal household chores and the empty fridge can be simple and totemic reminders of the resentment that often builds up and simmers under the surface as the balance of power shifts subtly within a relationship once children invade what was a previously harmonious dual-earner-couple existence. There must have been rubbish and washing then, but somehow I never noticed it until I had children.

The sociologist Professor Jonathan Gershuny, who has spent many years delving into how couples share out domestic duties, once described this process as a modern-day fairy tale, Allerednic (Cinderella in reverse). In this unhappy fable the prince and princess are two individuals with good career prospects until the prince marries the princess and turns her into a scullery maid by getting her pregnant.

In a lecture in 1999 he explained: 'And of course it's downhill all the way. She comes back to work. It's a strain because he hasn't got used to the childcare and she still has to take all the organisational responsibilities and so on … and in the meantime the other women's husbands in her department have been working hard and performing well, rightly, and get the promotion that she wanted. Her wages lag behind her husband's. So when they discuss the pressure they're under it's only rational that she cuts back on her paid work while he works extra hours which means in turn that the performance gap widens, perhaps she accepts the inevitable, decides she has other priorities than a career, and drops out altogether.'

Sound familiar? The chances are that the relationship probably isn't quite equal to start with. Girls tend to choose different subjects from boys at A level and university, often move into 'gender-specific' jobs that are usually more poorly paid, often known as the five Cs – cleaning, catering, caring, cashiering and clerical. Fewer end up in management positions than their male counterparts, and the gender pay gap – the gap in the average hourly earnings of men and women

– is still stuck at about 17 per cent, giving a clear incentive for the lower earner to quit first if the pressure of having two full-time jobs in the family home becomes intolerable.

But perhaps as importantly, the rapid pace of social change outside the home over the past half century hasn't quite been matched by a domestic revolution. In the 1950s men's and women's roles were defined: men were the employed breadwinners, women were generally the unpaid domestic homemakers and, usually, the recipient of an allowance from their husbands. Many assumed that as women moved rapidly into work in the second half of the century the traditional roles behind closed doors would also dissolve, leaving more equal partnerships all round. It wasn't to be, though.

Evidence from the British Household Panel Survey and countless studies in which families are given 'time use' diaries show that as women move into employment, the amount of housework they do does decline, but slowly, and the amount of housework that men take up is proportionately much less. The UK 2000 time use survey suggested that women spend on average three hours a day on housework (excluding shopping and childcare of which they do more than men too), whereas men spend about one hour forty minutes.

Two in five men do no ironing or laundry, whereas the number of women who do neither is around one in twelve. The only area of domestic work in which men out-perform women is DIY, but even this excludes gardening and decorating where roles are more evenly split. In couples where both partners have full-time jobs the husband is doing about one-third of the housework to the female partner's two-thirds.

As Gershuny, one of the analysts of the BHPS, explains: 'When women enter the labour force they do not lose their differential unpaid work responsibilities. Responsibilities that were separate but equal become joint but unequal.' Sociologists call this the 'joint burden'.

The arrival of a new baby doesn't just have a consequence in terms of job satisfaction or employment status but can also put an overwhelming strain on what may already be a fragile equilibrium at home. Some estimates suggest the arrival of a child trebles the amount of housework. Not only has this tiny, all-powerful creature changed your identity and your attitude to work for ever, shattered the cosy intimacy of life at home and demanded the lion's share of the love and attention you would have previously devoted to each other, but he or she has the power to create hitherto unimaginable volumes of washing and other chores. All those meals you might once have eaten out or on the hoof while working now require shopping, cooking and washing up and, as for the nappies, well they're just one of many new items that start filling the black bags.

American writer Susan Maushart in her book *Wifework* says that most couples start out with good intentions to share all the household tasks.

'Yet over time – usually a very short time – something happens to those good intentions. New mothers and fathers emerge from the haze of baby shock to find themselves behaving like something out of a 1950s sitcom. Suddenly he goes to work and brings home the bacon. She stays at home, frying it and feeding it to junior. "It's only temporary," they tell each other. Yet by the time she's ready to rejoin the workforce, the pattern has been set in concrete.'

The full scale of the task usually doesn't sink in until you are back at work. Gill was pregnant and sharing a substantial mort-gage with her boyfriend by the time she was twenty-one, having left school at sixteen for a clerical job in the city, which involved a daily commute from Essex to London. Even though she loved being at home with her daughter, financial pressure meant she was back at work by the time Lauren was nine months old.

'I used to meet up with my friends, we would go to the leisure club, do the step class, I could shop every day for fresh food and I felt like a real mum. It was an absolute joy and if I look back at photos from that time you can see I am ecstatically happy but the reality was that we had a mortgage to pay and we were going under really so I went straight back into work, doing as much overtime as possible so we could be financially secure.

'I would work weekends and whenever else they wanted me to do extra hours. I felt it was about keeping the whole family afloat because my boyfriend couldn't raise his earnings any more, so we wouldn't have survived otherwise. And in one sense it was very satisfying. I was a much better employee after I went back, and I know I did my job well; I had a new sense of purpose because I had to get promoted to get the pay rises and bonuses I needed.'

It was, she says, like a 'rat on a wheel' existence. 'Lauren's dad worked locally so he was able to help out at home but he didn't have the commute that I had, which had almost killed me off. Nor did he have the second job ... by the time I got home I was exhausted but then I would start washing, cooking, cleaning and ironing, often not even daring to sit down because if I sat down I would never get up again, so I had to somehow keep moving.

'I never really thought about my career. I just thought about paying the bills and our relationship probably was affected by the extra work. Eventually I stopped enjoying the job and my relationship with Lauren's dad was not working out. When you have a child, you should have a family life and that wasn't really happening so I just thought I have to change everything. Lauren was about four and a half. I know it coincided with her starting school and I went and moved in with my sister.'

In fact Gill changed more than just her personal situation; she went on to take A levels, went to university to gain a degree and is now a qualified solicitor. Financial independence gave her the power to leave an unhappy relationship but her unmanageable work-life balance also played a part in its failure. Even though she is now great friends with her former partner and they share care of their daughter, she admits that if she were to have more children she would want to work part-time in the early years of their life.

'If I went back full circle, having the qualifications I have now got, my priority would be to create a work-life balance. First time round I didn't have the luxury of being able to have emotions about that situation, there was nothing I could do, there was no one to complain to and I certainly wouldn't have turned around to Lauren's dad and said you are not providing enough for us because I want to work part-time, I wouldn't have dreamt of saying that. I just thought I have the potential to keep this family afloat and I have got to do it.'

The alternative to a cripplingly stressful dual burden at home and work might be to renegotiate a less stressful job, work shorter hours or drop out altogether, as Allerednic did, opting for 'wifework' rather than a career. But that too can come at a cost, especially if you are young, still feel you have ambitions, are struggling to 'fit' your new identity as a mother and maybe are the first in your friendship group to have children, so feel a relative failure.

Beverly's reluctance to put her child in a full-time nursery in the

early months left her no option but to give up a career she loved
as a lab-based research scientist. Flexible working wasn't an option
in a job that required long hours to finish experiments and record
data. She developed post-natal depression and also an unexpected
and bewildering resentment against her husband.

'I was very resentful because I just felt that, you know, the man's
life doesn't change at all, he just carries on as normal. Off he went
to work and I had to change my entire life.

'It was complicated though, because I wanted to look after the
baby and I didn't really want him to be at home with the baby. But
I also wanted his life to suffer, I wanted him to feel the impact of
the child but he didn't feel it. He was still travelling a lot when my
second child was born so I was still doing all the sleepless nights on
my own and I think it all just festered a little bit for a couple of years.'

Now that the couple are more settled and she has a new career
as an academic fund-raiser she feels less 'annoyed', but the domestic responsibilities are still shared unequally, something she is now
resigned to. 'It's really difficult because if the children are ill, it is
always me that has to miss work. He never has to.'

Feeling resentful is not an erratic emotion. Running her own
interior-design business from home did allow Angela to spend more
time with her young daughters after she gave up her job in the
pharmaceutical industry. 'My business is just more flexible and
works around everybody. My husband's out on the road, but even
if I wanted to, I couldn't realistically work any other way. But I do
feel sometimes that because I'm at home it's expected that I'll do
this and do that and pick the children up. It is silly to feel angry
about it, because I am here and he is not so it can't really be any
other way, but it doesn't stop you sometimes feeling a bit resentful.

His job is more important because it brings in more money and he runs it on his own with two other chaps and they're all over the country, but my job is still important to me, even if it doesn't bring in as much money. I still have deadlines to meet which means I sometimes have to work at the weekend because doing everything else means I can't get on with it during the week.'

For some women the realisation that they are living with an unreconstructed traditionalist doesn't really hit home until the children arrive, they are at home on maternity leave and the full weight of the increased household burden becomes apparent. For Eve, the shock of becoming a working mother at forty was compounded by the realisation that her husband, with whom she had previously lived a relatively carefree life, was at heart 'a bit of an old-fashioned boy, who had been quite closeted and spoilt himself'.

'I don't think you know what your husband is going to be like until you have children. He laid down the rule that the kids weren't going to go to nursery because they were going to be in institutions for the rest of their lives and he wanted a nanny, which was super-expensive. So we got a nanny and that completely wiped out my wages. I then didn't really have choice but to work full-time because we needed the money.

'I was really stressed trying to get up to speed on a new job and I had my husband on my case all the time. He was never very confident with the kids when they were babies and didn't help me at all. The job was quite a lot of responsibility and it was stimulating but after three months I said I can't do this any more and I was running everywhere, to work, back home, expected to go to book launches in the evenings and it just got impossible to juggle everything. I didn't resent the job but I resented my husband's lack of support.

'The resolution to that, though, came at the end of the year when I resigned and then he was happy. We had a very difficult year after that, our relationship suffered. I was very angry with him because it was a very good job for me, and if he had been a bit more flexible it could have worked out.

'I don't like being economically dependent on him, I find that quite scary, and I remember my mother always said to me I would have left your father a long time ago if I had been economically independent. We have talked it through and he says he is sorry now about the way things happened. I'm not sure our relationship would survive without the kids, but then we wouldn't have had any of these problems in the first place. I really admire women who do it all and don't get angry.'

It may sound far-fetched to suggest that something as weighty as women's chances of fulfilment, promotion and their ability to balance work and home should come down to matters as banal as the laundry or the shopping. But women who do have partners willing to share some of the domestic burden, who manage good, frank communication about how the various roles and responsibilities can be negotiated from the start, even before their maternity leave has ended, and couples who find time to show appreciation of the efforts each partner makes, seem to negotiate their way through these choppy waters more easily.

Rachel acknowledges that she would never have managed to keep her job as a hospital consultant without the support of her husband, particularly with the children. 'He would say that if I became a full-time housewife, life would be a misery. It would drive me mad. The children are in a nursery, breakfast and after-school club from eight to six and my husband always drops them off and picks them up. He is very reliable. I always feel that I am not giving enough at work, because by and large people who do medicine work all the hours there are.

'But Robert has very different views on working which is that, you know, you try and contain your work and organise it in such a way that you get it finished in the time that you have available and occasionally might need to do a bit more. We do online shopping but my husband will buy odds and ends because he has a lunch break and I don't because I'm in the hospital.

'I feel I am very lucky in the husband I have and most of the other women doctors I know only cope because they have husbands outside medicine who help them with the childcare. I think I've only ever had to pick up or drop off my children three times in the past five years and the women I see struggling are often those with partners who give them very little support.'

If there is the stirring of a slow cultural change in the way couples share the dual burden, it is starting with childcare. Men may not be champing at the bit to do more laundry but they are gradually increasing the time they spend with their children. Three-quarters of fathers now say they would like to be more directly involved in their children's lives. In families where both parents work, full-time fathers are now estimated to be doing around three-and-a-half hours a day on childcare in the week and between six and seven hours at weekends, about three-quarters of the time spent by mothers.

More men are taking paternity leave and, although the numbers are still small, more fathers are also asking to work flexibly (three times as many in 2005 as in 2002) which may be the start of a virtuous circle drawing fathers into an earlier and closer relationship with their children which will eventually lead them to make new demands on their employers.

In her book *Hard Labour* sociologist Caroline Gattrell examined the day-to-day reality of a diverse group of professional couples who were sharing work and family responsibilities to different degrees. She argues that while men are now prepared – and may even be relieved – to be sharing the 'breadwinner' role, if it reduces the pressure they feel as sole financial providers, they may also now be compensating for their loss of economic power by wanting to become more actively involved with their children, though this may still amount to 'cherry-picking' the time and activities they share. In a newspaper interview following the publication of her book she observed that 'Men's desire to have an equal parenting role does not extend to child-related domestic chores such as washing clothes or packing lunchboxes'. However, this does mean that increasing numbers of working mothers may be able to rely on their husbands in this one area at least, even if it is often the most enjoyable and rewarding bit of domestic life. Caitlin has worked either full-time or four days a week since her children were born but still depends on her husband, who works from home, to fill in especially where parental involvement at school is required.

'By the time the girls started school he had packed in his job and was running his own business from home,' she explains. 'He has his office at home where he shuts the door but he does work funny hours so if one of the girls says to him, "Dad, we're going to make rockets at school today – can you come?" he'll go with them, which means he may then have to work all evening. He's been to Shakespeare with the kids with the school and on other trips. He even went to the Isle of Wight for a week at the start of year six because they really struggle for men to go. I think the flexibility of work has changed; there are more dads around these days at the school gate, on the school's governing body and even the PTA.

'I know the girls would sometimes like me to be the one that goes but I think it is great that he can be there for them. They are very lucky to have a father who gets involved and it does make me feel less guilty about missing out on bits of their school life. And he doesn't feel he has been compromised, ultimately. He's an IT person who didn't want to become a manager, so he's ended up working for himself.

'However, he does draw the line at the less rewarding domestic chores. He doesn't do any cooking, or any washing and he very rarely does the ironing. If I plonk a basket of washing in front of him and say, "Can you sort that out," he'll sort it out – but you do have to ask him to do it.'

These more proactive late 20th-century fathers, known as 'Generation Y' (born after 1980), who unlike their baby-boomer predecessors may have grown up in homes where mothers worked, and who probably also have partners with jobs, have been carica-tured in the media as engaged in the 'daddy wars', both in conflict with their employers for better work-life balance and with their wives and partners for an equal share of the emotional relation-ship with their children.

The importance of work-life balance is slowly rising up the list of priorities that new graduates highlight when asked what they are looking for in a prospective employer. But until flexible working options complement higher status, rather than conflict, with well-paid management jobs, they are likely to be overridden by the higher priorities of career development and salary.

However, the growing recognition among men that there may be a desirable trade-off between work and a more fulfilling, less hurried emotional relationship with their children can't be ignored. The fact that fathers often feel they can't achieve that may partly justify the controversial assertion by the economist Catherine Hakim that women do have more choices than men. Some women find that prioritising family life over career does bring fulfilment and a better sense of balance in their lives, as Tessa found when she gave up her full-time career as a civil servant for a more flexible job locally when she and her family moved to the country.

'Even though I did try going back to work full-time I realised that my image of myself was not to be this successful career woman but to be a good mum really. I know that is sad and the wrong thing to say but it is true. The most devastating thing my son ever said to me was that they were talking about parenting at school and the teacher asked what makes a good mother and he wrote "always being at home and doing everything for you". But they never ask what makes a good father.'

The changing balance of power in the family also ushered new and different conflicts into the home. 'We agreed that I was going to perform the more traditional roles because my husband didn't want to come home from London at eight at night and do the dishes. And although there were regrets, because it set down a pecking order in the household, every choice has its upside. I see the kids and he doesn't. The advantage for me is that when they have problems they will chat to me, they won't chat to him. You can't have it all, you know.

'We have had rows in the past where he has expected us all to change when he walks through the door and for the children to become the perfect family, you know like "Dad's home, let's all do what he wants".

'I hear that from other families where we are, where the dad works in London all week and at the weekends they want to see their kids, but the kids want to go off and hang around town, and the dad starts saying, "I never see them when I'm home, they're always out."

'And to be honest I don't envy his lifestyle. I think he probably envies me more than I envy him because he sees me lounging around, chatting to the neighbours and knowing everybody. He often says he would swap roles. I think he would like to work fewer hours when he is older.'

But for every piece of research providing a glimmer of hope that assumptions about traditional roles within the home may be shifting, there is another to remind us how far we need to go. Even though three-quarters of fathers say they would like to be more directly involved with their kids, two-fifths also said they saw their childcare role as 'supportive' rather than 'hands-on' and a third still felt the breadwinner role was the most important aspect of fatherhood. Recent research at Cambridge University appears to suggest that a majority of British people now believe a mother's place *should* be in the home (but not necessarily that they want it to be) and that the idea that women *can* have an equal role in the workplace is a myth. One of the authors, Professor Jacqueline Scott, explained: 'There is clear evidence women's changing role is viewed as having costs for both the women and the family. It is conceivable that opinions are shifting as the shine of the super-mum syndrome wears off.'

Needless to say an otherwise serious report was accompanied

by the usual headlines, 'Superwomen are a myth', 'Women find it harder than ever to juggle work and family life,' and 'Family life suffers with working mums', none of which accurately sums up what the report actually said, but they served their purpose. As Professor Scott herself noted: 'Women – particularly mothers – can experience considerable strain when attitudes reinforce the notion that employment and family interests conflict.'

The fact that this research emerged at a time when record numbers of mothers are going back to work only serves to buttress the powerful assumptions that still exist about women's roles both at work and in the home. Even though the polling evidence now suggests that fathers want to be more involved with their children, public perception, at a time when there is also growing anxiety about children's well-being, is still that the child's welfare is the responsibility of the mother.

Working mothers are an easy target for blame when things go wrong, as if fathers have no role to play in their children's upbringing. The lazy headlines also overlook the fact that there are many other countries where children *are* judged to be happier and more high-achieving but where as many, if not more, women work, but in careers that are underpinned by more supportive policies for families and children.

In some ways we appear to be stuck at a point at which the relationship between men, women, work and children could go either way. It seems unlikely that working mothers are willing or able to give up work, whether they do it full- or part-time, whether they are career women reluctant to give up their hard-earned professional status, or doing jobs they are less wedded to simply to pay the mortgage and get by.

But unless there is a huge breakthrough in terms of sharing work and domestic responsibilities more flexibly, which would help women to continue jobs that keep them on an economic par with their partners, they seem destined to either become the scullery maids or carry on bearing the dual burden – along with the resentment that can bring.

The alternative virtuous cycle identified by Caroline Gattrell, in which new fathers desire to be more involved in their children's lives may start to change attitudes at home and in the workplace. But that may only happen according to the new generation of equality campaigners, if we acknowledge that some of the advancements in women's rights, in both maternity leave and in the workplace, may be counterproductive.

Women may appreciate the chance to fully bond with their babies, to reach the point where they feel keen to go back to work rather than being dragged back before they are quite ready and then negotiate part-time hours. But do those rights simply entrench underlying assumptions about women's traditional roles while simultaneously making employers more suspicious of female candidates with their entitlements to maternity leave and flexible working? The exemplar employers are certainly growing in number and many are now waking up to the demands of Generation Y male employees. But for every one – and they are often large employers – there is another often running a small or medium-sized business who seems more in tune with the attitudes of *The Apprentice*'s Sir Alan Sugar.

The long-term solution could be to offer fathers equal rights to parental leave rather than simply giving mothers maternity leave and then expecting them to transfer it to their partners, which can now happen but rarely does. This would allow couples to share their leave, possibly after the first six months so mothers could have the chance to wean their babies gradually. The recently formed Equalities and Human Rights Commission has argued that only this will start to change the culture of the workplace and help the bread-winner/homemaker stereotypes to disappear. Both parents would begin to feel more responsible for sharing childcare and other family responsibilities, men would start to inch towards wanting to work flexibly and employers would be forced to recognise and acknowledge this.

But the change could be slow. Finland has had 'non-gendered' parental leave for more than thirty years but only now do a majority of fathers take some paternity leave. In other Nordic countries where parental leave entitlements have been in use for some time, the fact that men still earn more than women appears to favour the mother making use of it unless men continue to be paid at the same rate as they would be at work.

Even then, fathers tended not to take up their entitlement unless 'father quotas' were introduced so that the leave is lost altogether unless it is taken by the father. This requirement helped to signal in an otherwise male working environment that the father was not being 'soft'.

Yet even in the Nordic countries, with generous leave schemes and highly subsidised childcare, women still gravitate towards less well-paid jobs in the public sector where maternity rights are better and, while housework appears to be more equally shared, work-life 'conflict' – the extent to which work clashes with domestic life – still exists.

Researchers studying international trends in family life in Sweden, Norway, Finland, France, Portugal and the UK looked at who actually did the laundry, shopping, cooking and caring for sick relatives in all six countries and tried to measure the extent to which exhaustion from work impeded a happy family life, and exhaustion from home made women poor workers.

They found that even though the Nordic countries were streets ahead in their progressive family policies and were achieving a better work-life balance, work-life conflict still existed. In France, also known for its generous childcare and support for working mothers and where over 50 per cent of women work full-time, 'work-life conflict' was high and on a par with Britain where less support for working families existed.

The academics concluded that the strong culture, which still exists in France, of women maintaining their traditional roles within the home even if they were working, still trumped anything the politicians could engineer.

This suggests that even with more progressive parental leave, shared or not, the role models we have grown up with still exert a powerful influence and that more legislation may be meaningless unless parents up and down the country start to provide different role models to their own children to help them escape the stereotypes.

Putting dads on six months' paternity leave may start to influence that, but unless the shift in domestic responsibilities is sustained after the parental leave period finishes, so that men continue shopping and cleaning and boys learn to iron and to cook so couples don't slip back into the same old routines, it simply won't work and will continue to lead to what one group of British and American academics, studying how couples adapt to changing work patterns, describe as exit (either out of the relationship or the job), voice (negotiating a more equal share of the domestic work) and suffering (just putting up with it). Their conclusion was that lasting change would only come if couples were eternally vigilant, to avoid them slipping back into old learned patterns of behaviour.

'If a husband has a habitual route to the living room from the front door and the wife to the kitchen, changing these requires continuous effort, a minute-by-minute awareness of the implications of each activity for the mutual balance of activities. The skills of domestic production are only gradually built up (e.g., the husband may not know how to operate the washing machine or sort the clothing for best results).

'And the meaning of participation in the various domestic activities may inhibit the agreed action (e.g., the wife may feel that by reducing domestic work she is failing as a woman).'

Even if such a conscious effort is made, the changes may take another generation or two. As someone who has failed miserably at 'domestic democracy', I remain sceptical that it will ever happen on a grand scale or, indeed, that all women will want to relinquish control of their 'domestic arena' at the same rate as their partners will want to enter it – unless they never took control in the first place.

Having lived for over twenty-five years with someone who still can't start the washing machine, load the dishwasher in any way that could possibly allow the dishes to be cleaned, doesn't do light bulbs, fuses, flat tyres, and once told me, when I suggested that he might mow the lawn, that if he had wanted to mow lawns he would have become a gardener, I am fully acquainted with the dual burden.

My own father bought me an electric drill for my 30th birthday (not a joke), fed up with being summoned for every small DIY job that needed doing, and realising that no one else in the house was going to learn how to hang pictures or put up shelves. But have I done anything about it? No. Most of the time I was just pathetically grateful to live with someone who is a great father, who did change nappies, get up in the night, stand for hours at the swings and on the touchline in freezing weather and bust a gut to get home from any number of professional crises to attend a parents' evening.

Yet it is with increasing alarm but not much surprise, if I am honest, that I have watched our elder son, in many other ways an admirable young man, regularly drive a full washing basket from Oxford to London only to leave it poised by the washing machine until one of the various women in his life – mother, girlfriend or doting granny – empties and recycles it for him to take back.

It is probably only the sheer physical distance between his younger brother's university and home that prevents him from doing the same. Both are adamant that they would want a working partner when they have children, say they loved their two main carers, claim to have very few negative memories of the long periods when we both worked full-time and those were more to do with the fact that the negative tensions around the job eventually spilled over into our home life.

However, both are brutally frank about the role models we have given them and attribute what they describe as their 'politically incorrect' views about women to the way we brought them up. My younger son told me recently: 'You basically made us believe that that is the way it worked, because you were always cooking the food and Dad was always coming in late from work. In terms of domestic stuff we were always much more dependent on you. I found it a lot more helpful to have my mum around, because my dad is just not practical and in that sense you satisfy the stereotype of parents.'

The fact that my elder son's girlfriend, who says her own parents manage a much more equal share of the domestic burden, is still willing to do his washing doesn't augur well for the future. If their generation of undergraduates, doing challenging degrees and determined to be equals at work, aren't sharing out the housework, it could take until the second half of this century before we resolve who does the laundry.

The writer Melissa Benn once described the working mother carrying the dual burden as the 'married lone parent'; a new breed of woman, who is 'not so much having it all as doing it all and has even become stripped of feminist idealism because she is so busy on her mobile trying to fix doctor's appointments, mopping her kitchen floor at midnight or checking her work emails after Newsnight'.

Being a married lone parent can be a lonely role. It is not dissimilar to managing a small enterprise, which may be why women who go back to work are so good at it. It is also a role that confers an alternative source of power and control that some women are unwilling to give up. When Lisa was going through childcare difficulties and had to sack her children's nanny, she found her husband fairly supportive but also decided it would be 'more complicated' if he got involved.

'I was working and I had employed her and he would help out if he had to and if it was an emergency, but I had to do all the negotiation and stuff, which in a way I preferred,' she explains.

And Sangita, a local councillor and senior manager in the voluntary sector with a long daily commute, still feels compelled to do the ironing at midnight. 'The staying up until midnight doing the washing and ironing is the really difficult bit. I see it as a whole badge of something, the ironing has to be done, it all has to be done, I hate thinking that we can't manage to do it all. I suppose I catch my own guilt that my child is well looked after and not suffering.'

She says her husband, while happy to play his part in the child-care, doesn't share her compulsion that her son should either eat the right organic food or have an ironed shirt or be as well turned out as the other little boys in his nursery.

Looking back now I can see that I had an underlying sense of panic that if I didn't control the domestic sphere when I was working, everything would fall apart. This, of course, played into the rest of the family's desire to do as little as possible and bluntly, as long as there was food in the fridge, they didn't care very much about whether the laundry basket or the bin were overflowing whereas it would drive me mad, particularly on arriving home after a long day at work when the only thing I wanted to find was order and calm.

Over the years I have lost count of the number of times I have found myself thinking, 'This time I really will insist they should sort their own odd socks or wash their empty cups and put them away,' only to calculate rapidly that it would be quicker and more effectively done if I did it myself. I daresay leaving them in a sea of dirty mugs and plates for days might eventually propel them into some sort of action, but the fact is that, conditioning or not, I have a lower tolerance of mess than the rest of the family and a greater need to know that everything at home is running smoothly. That may be an antidote to the chaos and stress that working can bring but the idea that I might have squeezed in a quick ironing lesson with my two sons at the end of the day when I was working full-time seems laughable – my teenage daughter, by contrast, has taught herself how to use the iron and also regularly cooks her own dinner.

Will we ever be able to stop ourselves ironing at midnight or be able to persuade men that it matters enough for them to do it? Just floating the idea that putting dads on paternity leave would eventually change the culture of women and work with two friends recently, both feisty professionals in every other way, left them incredulous. One, a full-time lawyer whose husband also worked at home, and mother of different-sex twins, argued that after ten years of observing them she was more than ever convinced that gender differences, when it came to caring and domesticity, were innate rather than down to centuries of conditioning.

No one has yet proved a genetic cause for this and most of us probably know men who share some cooking and shopping as well as doing increasing amounts of childcare. But examples of countries which have tried radical experiments to mitigate differences between the sexes, like in China and the kibbutzim in Israel, have only been partially successful. Both attempted complete equality between the sexes in terms of jobs and pay, but have eventually adapted to men and women doing different jobs and in some cases reverting to more traditional roles, especially once the kibbutz children were brought in from the communal houses to live at home with their parents.

A survey of Chinese men and women in the 1990s, almost half a century after the Principles of Equality were enshrined in the Chinese Marriage Law, found that even among the most educated professional groups in Beijing, where women earned the same or more as men, had access to good childcare and only one child, around a third of women said they would prefer to stay at home if they could afford it.

Liz describes the ease with which she 'fitted into the cliché', giving up her job as a solicitor in favour of a part-time job in a Citizens Advice Bureau so she could spend more time with her teenage children. 'I wouldn't necessarily have predicted that we would be where we are. We started out broadly equal and even when the children were babies my husband was very hands-on, pacing the landing on those awful nights and walking through the door after work and just grabbing a baby.

'But the truth is that I'm quite a contented person and happy to spend the whole day just pottering around the kitchen listening to Radio 4 whereas he needs to be busy. He is one of those guys that will have to think very hard about retirement, whereas vegging out with Delia Smith and *Desert Island Discs* is fine for me.'

The only sticking point for her is the mismatch in financial power and the couple still go through what she describes as an 'interesting' ritual with their joint finances.

'He said, "Why don't we just have a joint account now?" but I have always had my own salary and wanted to keep my own bank account so he solemnly gives me a cheque every month, which gives me an illusion of some sort of independence and is also farcical in a way because I know the money comes from him since I earn hardly any.

'I can also argue rationally with myself that with all my qualifications I should be doing more and that it is a waste for society that I am not, but am I unhappy about it on a personal level? No. Not even remotely bitter.'

Ingenious attempts to use the law to change the men's behaviour at home are still being tried. Only months after the BBC's *Woman's Hour* ran a spoof April Fool item suggesting that the European Union was going to make housework compulsory for men, the Spanish government tried a more subtle modern approach by introducing a new marriage contract for use in civil ceremonies which obliged men to share household chores, child-care and responsibility for elderly relatives. Some commentators noted that it may be hard to implement in a country where half of the men admit to doing no housework at all. But men who shirk stand to lose their rights in a divorce settlement if the couple part. Legislating for what goes on behind closed doors may seem draconian but nudging men towards more parental leave and job-shares may prove meaningless if it is not accompanied by fair shares of chores at home as well.

In an ideal world women like Liz, who are happy to trade some career success and prospects for time at home with their children, should feel free to make that choice without reinforcing the stereo-types in and out of the workplace to such an extent that it prevents another woman from managing to stay in a job she wants, or causes such bitterness or sheer exhaustion that the relationship breaks down.

But that, too, may be avoidable if the resentment and anger, whether over the black bin bags or the absent husband, were offset by more consideration and respect for each other's chores. Ironing at midnight is a lonely task but if you are loved, recognised and thanked for doing it, it may not seem quite so bad.

The new American First Lady Michelle Obama is one of the most high-profile global role models for the working mother and has been frank about her need to work. 'Work is rewarding,' she explained to a magazine interviewer while on the 2008 campaign trail. 'I love losing myself in a set of problems that have nothing to do with my husband and children. Once you have tasted that, it is hard to walk away.'

But she was equally honest about how even one of the most illustrious international power couples still had to struggle and overcome the banal and often irritating minutiae of daily domestic life in the early years of their daughters' lives.

'If a toilet overflows we women are the ones rescheduling our meetings to be there when the plumber arrives ... I think every couple struggles with these issues. People don't tell you how much children change things. I think a lot of people give up on themselves. They get broken, but if we can talk about it we can help each other.

'I spent a lot of time expecting my husband to fix things but then I came to realise that he was there in the ways he could be. If he wasn't there, it didn't mean he wasn't a good father or didn't care. I saw it could be my mum or a great babysitter who helped. Once I was OK with that, my marriage got better.'

Maybe there is a lesson for us all in that. A good work-life balance also means making time to talk and try to understand how the dual burden looks from both sides, whether you are on the quest for the White House or trying to find that plumber in a sleepy English suburb. A million miles from the high-octane American political scene in her cosy terraced house in East Anglia, with her hands full of two under-threes, a job, good childcare support and a husband who is 'very very supportive', Emma admits that she was always very surprised when people split up after having children.

'But now I can absolutely understand why it would happen because the thing that gets pushed to one side is the adult time that you have with your partner. I think we could all possibly do that a little bit better. I get the childminder to look after the baby when I get my hair cut but I have now said to my husband that I would like her to take them both for half a day so we could just go and have lunch together because in the evening we are both so tired.'

The blurring of the domestic lines may only continue at a snail's pace and the era when dads regularly wield the iron and the mop may take another decade – or three – but if our children are able to see that the dual burden can be negotiated slowly and accompanied by good communication and appreciation and carry that on into their own adult lives, it may become easier to bear.

CHAPTER 8

Why Do It?

The have-it-all superwoman of the 1980s did us all a great disservice. Under the beady eye of Margaret Thatcher, who apparently slept four hours a night and believed that the battle for women's rights had largely been won because she had managed to raise a family and become Prime Minister, many women of my generation were deluded into thinking that once they slipped into their padded-shoulders and walked out the front door, family life could be left behind and the workplace would embrace us.

It has been fascinating, heartening and depressing in equal measure to watch the gradual realisation that 'having it all' did really amount to 'doing it all' and was usually more exhausting rather than rewarding. The private and public conversations that followed have slowly become more honest. The opinion survey that suggested a majority of the public now think a woman's place should be in the home appears to reflect a new almost defeatist consensus that trying to manage work and children is impossible and the personal cost too great.

Would it be simpler just to admit we want to be parents first, to have time at home with the children, know the other mums at the school gate, get more involved in the children's education, be able to hang out at the swings for hours, and *always* be free for the school assemblies and doctor's appointments without having to rearrange work commitments to get there? Why do we worry about having an independent income and an identity outside the home that doesn't simply revolve around being a mother? Why not just live off someone else, or even on benefits, and cast off the hassle of 'work-life conflict'.

Maybe we are luckier than men, who are still struggling to feel it is OK to admit that they might like to work less and may find it easier to ask for an afternoon off to play golf than to take a child to the doctor or dentist. Maybe that 'perfect storm' of the right flexible job with money, status and prospects, a benevolent employer, warm, responsive, safe childcare and a partner who picks wet towels up from the floor is a pipe dream. There may be women that have all that, but I have never met them.

The reality of most working mothers' lives is a combination of the prosaic and the heroic. Whether they are ironing at midnight, getting up at six in the morning to make packed lunches before doing trips in opposite directions to a childminder and a primary school or overcoming a daily diet of headlines warning them that working mothers are bad for families, they usually show a resilience and determination that might make a lot of men blanch were they ever to be faced with the same imperfect storm of emotional and practical responsibility bundled up in a job that attracts no thanks or financial remuneration.

So why do we do it and what distinguishes those who make it work from those who don't? In the barrage of comment and criticism about whether women should be working, the fact that many women want and need to work is often overlooked. The average family is thought to need 1.5 incomes to survive. In spite of loving being at home with her first baby Gill describes the 'quite horrible' feeling of having to write to the building society and ask them to take reduced mortgage payments as the house she had bought with her partner sank into negative equity.

'The reality was that we had a mortgage to pay and we were going under and this deal with the building society was only for a limited period. So I went straight back into work full-time, doing as much overtime as possible so we got straight financially. I never really thought about my career, I just thought about paying the bills. I wasn't thinking, "I love my job and I want to get to this place" I just thought about paying the bills.'

Some children can't rely on two parents to provide. Their mothers are caught between a rock and a hard place, frequently caricatured as being 'less good' parents because they aren't part of a couple, self-centred and neglectful if they work, and damned as scroungers on benefits if they don't.

Nicky, the Welsh nurse who involved everyone from her granny to her school friends in the care of her only son so she could go back to work, admits she probably wouldn't have jump-started her career in nursing if she hadn't found herself in a damaging, disintegrating relationship with her baby son's father.

'I probably would have had longer off work, maybe the first two years. If money wasn't an issue, I may even have spent a good few years at home. But being with his dad, coping with what happened and going back to work made me a really strong person.

'I had one friend in particular who used to look after him a bit, but didn't work, and my son has asked me a couple of times why I have to go to work if some of his friends' mums don't. But her children had never been on a plane and she didn't drive so I used to say, "It's up to you Jake, I could sit at home, do nothing and not work but then we wouldn't have these nice things, a car and our own house and we wouldn't be able to go on really nice holidays to America and places like that." I think now he does appreciate it.'

Aspiration, the desire to make something of their lives and be self-reliant is still a strong theme that runs through the stories of so many women who continue working, whether or not they can rely on a second income.

'I do know everybody's circumstances are different and I was lucky in the fact that I was already trained before I had Jake,' says Nicky. 'And I do feel sorry for some of these girls who have babies and then say they can't work, maybe because they are not qualified to do anything. But I think it is good to show your children that if you do put your mind to it and work hard you can make something of yourself. I do want a better life for myself and my child, you know. I think my son realises that you can't sit at home if you want those things.'

It wasn't long after Nancy, a local government manager in Manchester, opened the post to discover her husband hadn't paid the mortgage for months that her marriage collapsed. The prospect of having her house repossessed appalled her, as did the thought of giving up her job. 'It was a miserable time, we had to sell the house and I lost nearly everything but I could never have given up my job because I would have felt as though I had no security and I wasn't brought up to live on benefits,' she explains.

The influence of our own mothers can be powerful and complicated. A survey of women before and after they became mothers, carried out by the Open University, discovered that the decision about whether or not to return to work and to use child-care, rather than look after their own children was one of the most stressful issues between mothers and daughters. This was especially the case when the daughters of stay-at-home mothers opted to work full-time or the daughters of working mothers opted to stay at home, generating feelings of rejection and failure on both sides.

'My mother worked because she wanted to,' explains Nancy. 'I don't think it was because my dad made her or anything like that. I went from my last day at school on a Friday straight to work in an office on the Monday. I am quite happy and proud of myself for what I have done, because I could have just lived off benefits, but that wasn't the way I was brought up, I would have felt that I had failed.'

Liz recalls some interesting discussions with her mother when she was a young mother going back to work as a solicitor: 'She had a degree and was a very bright woman who had worked in a bank for two years and then stopped and had babies and never went back because she was a great believer in small children needing their mothers. In my twenties I was coming from a much more clas-sically feminist position. I used to say to her that someone should have told me that having children didn't always fit with a career before I'd worked my wotsits off to get O levels, A levels and a rather tasty degree because I did know that I wanted to have chil-dren and she would just say, "Well, in that case, love, you don't need all those bits of paper do you?"'

Caitlin, who has worked throughout her children's lives, been an account manager in a number of large multinational companies and successfully challenged her employers when they threatened to downgrade her job on return from maternity leave, believes her own family background gave her immense confidence to pursue her career: 'I did a French and Business degree and it never crossed my mind that I would not work. I just wanted to have an interesting job. I come from a family of girls, my mum was a doctor, so I never felt that I wasn't going to work and I've never felt any pressure not to be able to do exactly what I wanted to do.'

Her husband's family's history of mental illness and depression, linked to stress, meant the couple, graduates and exactly the same age, each made a conscious decision to continue work. 'It was never an option for me to give up. I find it quite enlightening talking to other women who are both younger and older than me who still get told "the woman's place is in the home" or "you'll never amount to anything" and they suddenly feel like that's true. I was lucky because I knew that my husband never ever wanted me to stay at home.'

The part our parents play in either reinforcing aspirations or ambition is often inextricably linked to their, and our, education. When I read newspaper headlines proclaiming either that women want to, or should, stay at home with their children, two questions always immediately spring to mind. The first is whether the editors who write them are encouraging their own daughters to leave home at sixteen in preparation for marriage and a family. I would imagine the answer in most cases is that they are not, in fact quite the reverse; many will be educating their daughters in high-achieving schools in the full expectation that they will go to university, and get a good job rather than look for a suitable husband.

The second question, the answer to which we can't fully know, is how many women, faced with that 'lottery win' and freed from the financial need to work really would decide to stay at home and be full-time mothers, as some opinion polls appear to suggest.

Though we may still be conditioned to take the lion's share of the domestic chores, many of us are also the product of aspirant, determined working parents whose identities from a very young age have been shaped by the assumption that we would achieve something else outside the home, which is why I have my doubts that after the first few months at home (or out spending that lottery-win money) we would all still be 'doing nothing'.

Much of the research into the choices men and women of all ages make about their jobs suggests that the differences between the sexes when it comes to work commitment have been narrowing. This is especially true of younger people and those with higher educational qualifications, as more women contribute to the household income.

Even though committment to work may decrease as men *and* women get older, both have less to prove, more achievements to feel proud of and experience more financial security, it doesn't altogether vanish. Women may work less but they don't stop completely. Even now, for the first time in my life in the financial position where I don't need to work, and frequently lured by the prospect of lolling around at home listening to Radio 4 and brushing up on my cooking, I can't quite bring myself to stop doing *something*.

It is now an annual family joke among my children that every September, when I come back from holiday, I start talking about giving up work and learning French instead, then never do it. My sense of myself as an independent working person is impossible to shift, however irrelevant my contribution to the household income becomes, which may be in no small part down to my own mother who still does a part-time job as well as being an energetic school governor and a political activist in her early eighties.

It is partly a fear of losing that sense of financial independence, or rather being able to retain that feeling that you 'have your own money'. Loss of financial independence hurt Beverly almost as much as her husband's long absences and the loss of her career as a research scientist. It also contributed to her sense of isolation and depression after her daughter was born.

'We had always pooled rent or mortgage payments, I always had my own money so I was always independent, and then I had to go to having absolutely nothing. I felt very uncomfortable with that.'

But it isn't just about money. Many women will empathise with Liz's desire to be at home for her teenage children but also understand her wish to be able to tell people, if asked, that she does something, even if it is going down to the CAB every week in her jeans to do a small but interesting part-time job which still requires her professional knowledge. The illusion of independence that she and her husband collude with, as he puts money into her bank account every month, allows her to continue religiously paying her subscription to the Law Society, a simple totemic act which symbolises that she is also a professional and that all those 'bits of paper', the O levels, A levels and the degree, still mean something.

Jane stuck with her loathed, bullying, sexist employers while her children were small partly because she and her husband had bought a large house that required extensive building work. 'There was no question that I could stop work, the financial implications of that were huge, but even if we'd been absolutely rolling in it I would still have worked. I've got friends who have never worked since their children were born and they have no intention of going back until the children are older but that would never work for me. Work is a big part of my life and I know it's an old cliché, but I always felt, however awful it was, that at least I had something to come home and talk to my husband about.

'It never, ever crossed my mind that I would be doing the gardening, going to the gym and meeting up with the other mums for coffee, full-time. Obviously I used to enjoy my Fridays off with my friends, they were great, but I would really miss that other side of my life.'

The part that work plays in personal identity and self-esteem is too often overlooked in both public and private discussions about 'what women want'. One occasional policy proposal floated by politicians is that the state should pay women to stay at home with their children. Former Conservative Party Leader Iain Duncan Smith has called for a fundamental rethink of family policy to encourage all mothers to stay at home with their children until they are three, possibly funded by allowing mothers to take all their child benefit payments in the early years of their children's lives.

This, he argues, would help to reduce the risk of unhappiness and antisocial behaviour in older children, which he links directly to many parents' failure to form 'a close and loving relationship with their babies', singling out lone-parent mothers in particular. 'Society is paying a high price for the quick-fix of getting mothers back to work so soon after birth,' he claims.

It is hardly surprising that public opinion appears to be turning against the idea that mothers can work and have a happy family life. Sweeping statements about feckless children, a broken society and the selective use of evidence to back up what are, at best, unfounded assertions about the role of working mothers in social breakdown are becoming more common. They invariably exempt working fathers – especially those who choose jobs with antisocial and family-unfriendly hours like being a member of Parliament or a newspaper editor – from any responsibility for their children. However, there is no doubt that they fuel more panic and guilt.

They also overlook the longer-term consequences for women who do leave the job market altogether, lose confidence and skills and then find themselves less well off and possibly reliant on the welfare culture that the same politicians profess to despise or, if they are supported financially, feeling unfulfilled and demotivated.

Public debate in an era of fast, round-the-clock media is invariably simplified down to polar, and usually false, opposites, in this case full-time work versus stay-at-home motherhood overlooking the fact that while many women might relish the chance to spend more time with their children, whether they are four or fourteen, that does not necessarily mean they want to be full-time mothers. And why should they? Being at home with small children twenty-four hours a day doesn't just involve a loss of hard-earned skills. It can be boring and lonely as well.

Rachel, who became a hospital consultant shortly before her children were born, has consciously compromised some aspects of her job, no longer travelling abroad for meetings or agreeing to stay late at work. However, she admits that even on maternity leave she was anxious to be doing something else: 'It sounds awful to say it but I didn't find them that interesting when they were babies. I enjoyed my second maternity leave much more than the first one because I had an older child, so for me the older years are more interesting and it may be that as time goes by, work will become less of a driver and, if I had to, I'd go part-time.

'But I couldn't be a full-time stay-at-home mum. Even when I was on maternity leave I was starting to think that I should join a local organisation or become the secretary or something like that, and then I just thought that's insane! But the truth is I will always find something to do and so I might as well just stay in work. People choose to go into medicine not just because it is interesting and you can help people, but it is such an opportunity to take on other roles, education, management or research. Something different every day. What could I do that is any better than that?'

And women don't need to be affluent professionals or graduate high-fliers to crave intellectual stimulation outside the home. Nancy left school at sixteen and couldn't wait to get back to her job in local government: 'I was thirty-three when I had Iona. As she has got older I have enjoyed being a mum more but I won't stop working.'

Sangita did actually find herself going back to her commitments outside work, in local politics, when her son was a few weeks old. 'It *is* about needing an intellectual challenge. I mean clearly I adore my son but being at home all the time is very isolating. I needed to have that combination of home life with an outside interest. I didn't have that horrible feeling of getting very insular if I knew I had an important meeting in the evening. I didn't go to every meeting in that period but I would cart him around with me if I had to, even if the consequences were sometimes unintended.

'On one occasion a constituent was having a real go at me and the baby just projectile-vomited all over the place so I was covered in baby sick. He just didn't bat an eyelid while I was mopping rancid milk off me and the poor council officer had to scuttle off to get some tissues. To be honest, if I had been in a more senior executive position on the council, I probably wouldn't have gone back to work when he was four months old because I would have still had another challenge but I knew I needed something challenging to keep my mind going.'

Emma is equally unapologetic about wanting to go back to her job in science and medical publishing by the time her daughter was on solids and she had taken almost nine months' maternity leave. 'It sounds awful but no, I didn't feel bad about going back. I felt very comfortable with it. I just wanted to start thinking in a different way again. I felt I might go rusty and we were very lucky, the whole process was very smooth.'

And even though she eventually gave up her career to be at home while her son was doing his GCSEs, Liz couldn't have done it when they were younger. 'I suppose I didn't have to work, we could have carried on belt-tightening and not going abroad and living in a small house and all that, so I was in quite a choosy position.

'But I didn't like to be at home all the time. I'm not brilliant with babies, I think I like them an awful lot more for not seeing them 24/7. Also I was quite proud of achieving what I'd achieved in work and I didn't want to just jack it in. It had taken me two attempts to get my solicitor exams and, you know, it mattered quite a lot.

'I did decide when my son was six months old that I would look for something part-time. It's just the classic compromise, isn't it? I'll do three days at work and four days at home and I did have the freedom to apply for jobs and then turn them down if they insisted on someone full-time. So that was quite a nice situation to be in, but I still had this feeling of keeping options open.'

Sometimes doubts about going back to work can mean the benefits are unexpected and doubly rewarding. Clara, a psychology graduate who felt obliged to go back to her job in university administration to pay her share of the mortgage on a new family house, was worried about returning: 'The longer I was on maternity leave the more apprehensive I started to feel.' She was able to work three days in the office and a half day at home and keep her management post. 'I was determined not to go back until my daughter was ready but she settled in with the childminder very quickly and I actually appreciated having time to myself and going out at lunchtime without a pushchair. That is a freedom I wouldn't have had if I hadn't had to go back to work. Having a life outside of baby groups was nice, I mean I like them, but it was a relief. I thought before I went back that I might be quite happy being at home all the time but actually when it came to it, I enjoyed much more than I thought I would being back at work, and having a separate life.'

She believes being a mother has made her more effective at work, too: 'The job involves quite a lot of pressure, as there are changes taking place which require thinking through how we might work in different ways. I am aware that there are comments made about part-timers but I don't get to hear about them directly and I do feel satisfied that I have got the balance right. The really interesting thing for me is that, though I initially worried about having to leave on time, as I used to have the freedom to stay and squeeze a few more hours in, even though I am now at work for fewer hours I have more energy and motivation. I work more efficiently and I had never anticipated that. For example, I am now conscious that I can't just stop and chat with colleagues and I find myself apologising to people and saying I can't talk because I have to get on with my work.'

Some women go back to work because they don't feel as confident in their abilities as a mother as they do in their jobs. Before Tessa and her husband made the radical lifestyle change of moving to the country, she did go back to work in the civil service and remembers finding herself 'padded up to the nines and leaking milk everywhere' in a job interview which would lead to promotion. Even though it meant leaving her two-week-old son at home screaming the house down with his dad, she forced herself to do it because she feared what she might lose if she *didn't* go for it.

'They rang me up and said did I want to be promoted. I thought I can't miss out because at that moment I didn't feel good, I felt hopeless as a mother and I didn't have the confidence that I would be a good parent at all because having my first was a huge shock to me. I didn't know the first thing about babies. I had this powerful feeling for him which I hadn't planned for at all. I thought the baby would be nice and cute but the whole experience wasn't nice and cute at all, it was overwhelming. I just wasn't psychologically prepared and I thought I'd better not lose everything at this point, you don't get promoted that way.

'I got through the interview and got the job. They obviously didn't notice what a state I was in or that I was secretly thinking, "Don't you realise I've got this baby and I don't know what to do with it and all I do these days is change nappies." It was horrendous but I would really have taken it as a real blow if I hadn't got it.'

In fact Tessa went on to be a devoted mother and part-time worker, throwing in her Whitehall career for rural life and job flexibility. But admitting that full-time motherhood doesn't necessarily appeal to you isn't the same thing as being a bad mother. The resolute and spirited way so many women do go back to work might even help them become better mothers as well as better employees, if it makes them happier than they would be at home full-time.

And the phrase 'if you want to get a job done ask a busy woman' is never truer than when applied to working mothers, many of whom don't just work part-time but then also compensate for any loss of professional satisfaction by taking on a host of other hobbies or community activities.

Exhausted or not, that same urge to be 'doing something', feeling fulfilled and engaged often spreads its tentacles in that day off or the carefully engineered 'down time' especially if it is something that can be enjoyed with the children. Caitlin runs a Guides unit outside of her full-time job. 'Because I don't spend a lot of time with my girls it is something we can do together and I also play netball. I train on a Wednesday, I play on a Saturday morning, I've done that ever since I finished university and I'll never give that up. I refuse point-blank to. My husband moans about it sometimes but it's like no, this is me, this is my time, this is what I do and it keeps me fit.'

When Tessa gave up the Whitehall job she had been promoted to within two weeks of giving birth; she found a better work-life balance in a local job in the voluntary sector. But she also realised that it mattered to her to have time for herself. 'I used to get to Saturday and then have all these children waiting in a queue to be taken places and I realised I didn't get a day off and that I just needed to be on my own sometimes, have time at home when they are not here with no one there hassling me. I felt as though I was always on duty, like a school teacher.'

However, she quickly filled her spare time with being a secondary school governor and running a small livery yard next door to her house, which still allows her to pursue her love of riding. Clara keeps up the flute lessons and freelance writing that she started on maternity leave: 'I was desperate to use my brain for something or other and I think it is quite important to have something else of interest outside motherhood.'

Some women even set up and run businesses in their non-work time. Karen, is technically off-duty at home on a Friday and able to pick her son up from school, as part of the four-day week she negotiated with her physiotherapy practice. But she doesn't really have a day off because she and her husband also own several properties locally that they have refurbished and rent out.

'I love my job, wouldn't want to move and can't really get promoted from where I am now. Running the flats takes up a lot of free time in the week and sometimes at the weekend so I find that, even though I am only working at my job four days a week I often spend my Fridays sorting out things to do with the properties.

'There are some days when I think why are we doing this on top of everything else. If we didn't I would certainly have more free time. But it is interesting and fun and also an investment we will have when we stop working. I don't really have a spare moment, but I can't remember the last time I was bored or didn't have a list of things to do. It has all been very stimulating for me.'

The inner voice urging women to stay busy, keep their minds active, have something to talk about beyond their children, whether or not they need to contribute to the household budget, needs to be recognised in the public discussions for and against working mothers. Even if it only leads to small steps back into work and is followed by a period of chopping and changing jobs to accommodate maternity leave and subsequent children – and women are between two and four times more likely than men to enter or leave the labour market between the ages of twenty-five and fifty – the confidence that brings can breed confidence. Once the initial few years of juggling are established, many women have an ability to multi-task that eludes their male colleagues and sometimes makes it easier to try out new opportunities and adapt to new challenges.

Having left school without any qualifications and describing herself as 'not the sort of person to do O levels or GCSEs', Dee's bumpy journey in and out of work as she raised four children took her from being a bus driver to starting her own business. Opting to work for themselves is a choice made by increasing numbers of women who become disillusioned with the lack of flexibility of office life.

'I always wanted to write but you know coming from my background there weren't expectations that we would stay on at school or go to university,' she says. 'My mum and dad thought you got a good job and you worked at it for the rest of your life until you got a pension. To them, if you worked at the London Underground, that was a very good job. I remember my older sister got a job working on the Tube and didn't stick it and my dad went mad.

'They were very strict, very simple people and their idea of support was to say, "Go and read a book, make sure you behave yourself at school." We'd get into really terrible trouble if we gave the teachers any problems at school or anything like that. They did come to parents' evenings but I don't think they really knew what the options were. I remember going to the careers guidance meetings that you have when you're fifteen, sixteen and all I took away from that was that I could do hairdressing, catering or childcare.'

Driving a bus allowed Dee shift work which meant that she and her husband could share the childcare with a part-time childminder. Her ambition to achieve more, and to write, was always hovering in the background: 'I remember driving from one end of the route to the other. When I got to the other end I used to sit there with my notebook, writing down any interesting things that I saw.'

After a brief spell working as a classroom assistant in her children's school, Dee spotted an advertisement for a writing course and, after joining it, met someone who had a degree for the first time in her life. 'I remember sitting and speaking to her and she read the *Guardian* and I'd never looked at the *Guardian* because my dad read the *Mirror*. When I looked in the *Guardian* and I saw jobs for journalists, I thought wow. Then I discovered a university course that I wanted to do, did an access course and started my degree. I was either quite fortunate or blessed because by the time I was ready to go to university all of my children were fully at school, the youngest one was five and had just left nursery. They had a playcentre attached to the school, and I got a place for all of them.'

While at university her marriage broke up and she relied on friends as well for childcare: 'Sometimes I was able to stay in the library to finish an assignment rather than coming home. Studying with children means that you buckle down. You just don't mess about. I was a lot older than many of the other students so I just really got on with what I had to do. I really discovered that I had it, you know, and that I could do it. I was getting up to 75 per cent in my essays and the confidence that I got from that was immense.'

Dee started freelancing while still at college and before she finished had secured a job on a newspaper for the Jamaican community in London: 'It was full-time so I wasn't home after school. That's where the struggle was. As soon as I finished work, I had to run, then if there was a delay on the train and I was underground and couldn't ring, it was a worry. It was a very stressful year, but I did carry on.'

Avoiding the slow drift into a lower status, more poorly paid job after having children isn't easy as there are so few quality part-time jobs. But starting a small business can provide a stimulating alternative. Dee became an enterpreneur almost by accident, partly because her next job, editing a magazine for a large voluntary-sector organisation ended acrimoniosly: 'I had a horrible manager there. She was very efficient and I completely respected her professionally but she was horrible, really horrible. It wasn't personal, she was just mean. My daughter had eczema so she barely slept at night because she was so uncomfortable. It is only now when I look at pictures of her – she was like this big pink red raw thing – I realise how much discomfort she was in.

'But my manager would tell me off for doing things like calling the doctor to make an appointment or organise a repeat prescription. I'd try to explain that I couldn't call the doctor any other time because they closed at 11.30, but she was completely uncaring. She had no children and she was a bully. I wasn't the first person that she had driven out of the job and in fact the person that covered for me while I was on maternity leave didn't even turn up on the day she knew I was coming back, even though she was supposed to spend two weeks handing over to me. I think she'd just had enough.

'I started coming to work feeling really, really tired from being up at night with my daughter. I started to get headaches and eventually she gave me a written warning. I joined the union because I had already seen what she had done to another member of staff and there were quite a few people in the building who were fed up with her, including the shop steward. I appealed against the written warning and the union backed me and were very supportive which eventually helped to overthrow her allegations.'

Being moved to a different department didn't help Dee because there was no obvious role for her to fill so she was paid redundancy and that gave her the chance to do an MA in publishing. Part of her assignment was to look at educational publishing and also to do a business plan. This coincided with the start of the really challenging episodes in her son's education. 'He just wasn't grasping phonics, I don't know why; it didn't appear that he had dyslexia but he was not making progress. He was probably having a horrible time because I had been through a difficult divorce but, whatever the reason, it spiralled into behavioural issues and he wasn't learning or doing what he was supposed to do in the classroom.

'He used to stay in the home corner when it was time to stay on the carpet and got into the habit of taking his shoes off wherever he felt comfortable and then making a really big fuss about it but the school didn't like it. We got on well with the head teacher, but when they first mentioned that maybe he should have a statement, we just didn't understand what it meant. It sounded so horrible to have your child statemented. So I resisted because I didn't want that to spoil things for him later on. Eventually we started to understand what it meant and I found myself thinking that there must be many other parents like me who don't really understand what their role is and how they can support the school and, if there is a problem, how they can sort it out. That's when I got the idea for a magazine for parents who needed support in the way I feel I needed support, somewhere to go where you wouldn't feel intimated, where you didn't have to feel silly because you're asking questions.

'I wanted to create something that would give parents a safe, non-threatening environment where they could get answers. I felt all the magazines out there were aimed at teachers, not parents, so I thought it would be interesting to advertisers who wanted to reach parents. For me, there was an emotional reason for doing it.'

The rise of the so-called 'mumtrepreneur' has been quite dramatic over the past decade. The number of women working for themselves has leapt by nearly 20 per cent since 2000 and now tops one million. Often it is personal passions or interests that propel women out of jobs and into devising original ideas which can make them money and allow them to work flexibly. The IT revolution has made it much easier to nurture an idea and then start a business from home. There are now a wide range of organisations and websites offering advice on how to turn a personal passion into a viable business plan, how to raise money from formal loans, how to manage informal loans from friends and family and how to market yourself, sort out effective PR and grow.

Lynne Franks started her own PR company in 1971 which went on to become the third-largest consumer PR business in the UK. She now runs Seed Networking for Women, which offers advice and coaching for women who want to start their own businesses or work for themselves in order to get a better work-life balance.

'Women have a different way of using their brains; they are more intuitive, empathetic and better at communication,' she says. 'These are all-powerful business tools but women are often in denial about that if they are working in a man's world and it can get knocked out of them by the corporate structure. But it is very important that they do the right research and test the market if they are going to start up in business alone.'

Dee got a loan from Business Link to start her magazine, but also had help from her own mum: 'She was very supportive with bringing funds together to get the print done. I didn't have a lot of savings so it was really a family effort, but it was tough. I didn't realise how hard it would be to get the magazine sold and I was driving around in my husband's van, with my satellite navigation system telling me where to go and with piles of boxes in the back. I visited schools and education conferences and shows, taking my son with me in the school holidays and I was also freelancing three or four days a week for other publications to survive.'

Eventually the pressure of doing it all alone became overwhelming and Dee got an offer to merge with another, more established, parenting magazine that had a ready-made marketing and subscription structure. She grabbed it and became the editor of the new publication, no longer her own boss but finally achieving her teenage dream of being able to write and edit in a job that allowed regular hours, some control over her working life and the chance to be at home one day a week to pick up her youngest daughter, who goes to an after-school club for an hour on other days, from school.

Government research into the way British businesses develop suggests that women are more cautious and risk-averse than men about going it alone, which may be why so many prefer to start up by borrowing money from family and friends. They are also less likely to know anyone else with an entrepreneurial background, to see good business opportunities or to feel they have the skills to set up their own company.

Even if the start-up goes smoothly, moving on to the next stage brings challenges that may need outside advice and help. Former journalist Jane got her PR business off the ground quickly and in the way she wanted, so that she could adapt her work routine to her children, being free to take them to and from school. Going it alone was also a welcome break from being someone else's employee.

'There seemed to be very little flexibility with the person I was working for so I just thought, "Why am I doing this?" I think women often don't realise that the skills they have are transferable. I was a journalist and had always thought that is the only thing I could do. I found that my writing skills were a really useful commodity that other people wanted.'

She quickly attracted a core group of clients. 'It just grew and grew and grew and, after I realised how easily distracted I got working at home, I got a cheap and tiny little office around the corner from home, above an estate agent's. That meant I could take somebody on to help me and I now employ five other women. I have absolutely no regrets. Everything is really local apart from the times when I have to travel with work. Sometimes that's all a bit hairy, but then I can rely on other mums. I've never had any advice from anybody but just recently I've sort of thought, "Where is all this going?" I seem to be working five days a week, but after all my difficult experiences as an employee I do want to enjoy my work myself but also be a really good employer too. I also think it's very difficult for me to let go and maybe take on more staff.'

Giving up control and moving to the next stage of growing your own business is often the hardest stage for self-employed women, according to Lynne Franks. 'They often find losing control is very difficult but you can't keep control and get bigger. Women need help and advice about team-building and employing others. You can't just let the business depend on you.'

Angela started an interior design course after she gave up her full-time job to be at home with her daughters. While she was studying for her new qualification, she started to make curtains to bring in some extra money and the business took off. 'I started to make quite a bit of money then decided, right OK this isn't a hobby now, I need to inform the tax man, which was the point at which my business was born and it's just grown and grown. I've never taken a loan out from the bank or anything; I've learnt to manage the business on the way. Every year I've doubled my turnover. I'm very flexible, I could be working seven days a week, it could be five.'

But working for yourself can be lonely, not least because there is usually no one else to bounce ideas off. 'The thing I do miss, being my own boss, is being able to hand over to someone else or just having someone to talk things through with if I have a problem,' says Angela. 'I would like to make the business even more successful, I would love to have my own showroom or maybe a shop and expand but that would mean taking the plunge and employing someone else if I really want to take on any more work.'

According to Prowess, a web-based organisation that supports women entrepreneurs with advice, mentors and networking opportunities and offers links to local support networks, having the right start up idea is crucial. Women also need to be prepared for their work-life balance to get a bit out of kilter for the first few years until the business becomes established.

Prowess warns that women often fall into the trap of believing that they need to do everything themseleves, getting anxious if other people do help but not in quite the way they want. Prioritising, sharing the load and even planning time to take a break every day is essential. Women should take regular time out to work out where their business is going.

Jackie Brierton, who runs the Prowess National Policy Centre, says: 'There's undoubtedly more publicly-funded business support focused on women available now than there was five years ago, and a greater understanding that support needs to be delivered in a way which suits women's circumstances.

'They are often quite different from those of male-owned businesses – which are too often considered the norm – because for women what is important is getting the right kind of advice and support at the right time.

'The needs of women beyond the start-up stage are not differentiated enough from those of men and although you can certainly argue that their technical needs are not different – it's *how* the advice and support is delivered which is important and this continues to be the case as the businesses grow. There are also specific personal development needs, particularly linked to confidence-building, which many women prefer to be addressed in a women-focused environment.

'Research has shown that women particularly value the advice and help they can get from other women. Peer mentoring is one of the most effective ways to ensure women get through the start-up stage successfully and there are a number of websites that offer online peer support.'

Retraining, learning new skills or going back into full-time education, whether it is going back to university or doing a more practical vocational course that unleashes a hidden entrepreneurial or creative spirit, can be a vital part of making the change from full-time work to something more adaptable to children. When Gill's relationship collapsed under the pressure of a stressful job and long commute, she realised she was 'going to have to change everything'.

'I moved in with my sister so I didn't need any childcare and enrolled in the local sixth-form college, which is actually the college I would have gone to if I hadn't left school at sixteen. Living with my sister was great, she had a three-bedroom house and as far as Lauren was concerned I was a full-time mother because I still took her to school and picked her up and she could have her friends around and I didn't need any childcare.

'I was quite depressed to start with and the split from her dad was on my mind a lot but I was also quite motivated. I was doing voluntary work at the primary school two afternoons a week, swimming and reading with the kids, which I really enjoyed. The tutors liked having someone older in the class and I was working really hard so my grades kept going up and up.

'What was really interesting was that as I began studying seriously and putting as much effort into that as I had into my job, especially into English Literature and reading plays and poems, I began to learn an awful lot about myself and I started to gain proper confidence. For the first time in my life I was surrounded by people who were talking about going to university and my teachers kept telling me I should take it further, so that was the first time I thought, potentially, my God, I could go to university too.

'I started going into the library researching careers and thinking about going to do work experience. Then I got the Yellow Pages out and went through and started calling up local solicitors' firms.

'One small local firm asked me to come along and I just started working there for nothing, just for the experience; I think they used to give me lunch money, but gradually they started giving me a lot of responsibility. I started going to court; I was just clerking, but so many of the lawyers were women and it was completely inspiring see them all out there doing this incredible job. They were clever and witty and charming and I just thought, that is what I really want to do, not necessarily being a barrister but working at that professional level.

'They were my role models. One in particular had started as a secretary then began her own company. She went on to do a degree and was called to the Bar in her fifties. That spurred me on and I got three As in my A levels and applied to university to read Law.'

Thanks to a combination of help from friends and family, bursaries, student loans, bonuses left over from her days working in the city and 'applying for everything that was going', Gill managed to get her law degree, juggling study with motherhood: 'It is fair to say that I didn't have the typical university life with the drinking and the partying and going to clubs because I just wanted to get back and be with Lauren.

'I still took her to school every day, there were only a couple of days a week where I would need someone to pick her up when I had a lecture, but I felt I was working towards our future and I could still study while she was in bed. In fact she remembers this table being covered in books, you could never see it.'

Looking back, Gill sees the eight years that took her from being an unemployed bank clerk and single mother to a busy urban solicitor as evolutionary, guided as much as anything by her responsibilities as a parent and the changes that responsibility forced her to make.

'I certainly didn't start out thinking, right I am on an eight-year mission to become a lawyer, I just thought I have got all these years ahead of me, I want to be a good mum to Lauren and I want to be able to provide whatever she needs outside school. But I learned so much about myself on the way, and finding the confidence that I could do something more with my life *and* combine that with being a mum was an eye-opener and has already had an effect on her.

'She now thinks it is perfectly normal, and indeed expects, that she should go on and do A levels and go to university, so the opportunities that weren't given to me at first now seem like the natural order of things to her.'

It is still a juggle. A full-time career presents problems, like the day her daughter and her friends got over-excited and broke a window. Gill is heavily reliant on help from friends and family, her own parents, Lauren's dad and the sympathetic law practice in which she works to allow occasional flexibility.

'I did my legal practice course when she was in her first year of secondary school, I started work full-time when she was in year eight and I still have to be very organised and plan my work routine very carefully so I know that if I have to work weekends, she could be with her dad. I never want my employers to turn around and say I am shying off work because of childcare issues or that I called for their sympathy. I love the work; I know I am doing the right thing because I feel so motivated.'

The journeys from being a London bus driver to a small businesswoman and magazine publisher, or from being a school-leaver bank clerk to solicitor, may be exceptional examples of inspiring, unplanned, but upwardly mobile paths women can follow after they have children. But they do illustrate how, even though it may be only in a minority of cases at the moment, the changing priorities that children bring can also be accompanied by small, unplanned steps that are positive and fly in the face of the accepted wisdom that children necessarily mean downward occupational mobility.

Whether they emerge from that need to continue earning, the stimulation of a part-time job, the desire to have 'something else to talk about' and use your brain in a different way, or to get out of the house without a buggy, the confidence they bring can breed confidence. Harnessed the right way, those small steps may lead on to greater things and a better, not worse, work-life balance.

CHAPTER 9

After The Gap

What happens to the women who give up work altogether after they have children, joining what is often known as the 'hidden brain drain' or the 'mummy track' and can be a vicious cycle of broken work experience, lost confidence, low self-esteem and jobs that can undervalue skills and qualifications? Many of the women on it, and I was one, think that finding a part-time or flexible job is the answer when they are struggling to keep their heads above water and just want to do something to keep their hands in or earn a bit of extra cash. Only later, when looking back, does it become obvious that they have settled for jobs that pay less and offer fewer opportunities than their pre-baby employment.

One recent study suggested that one in three corporate managers switch to part time work and move down the occupational ladder when they become mothers, two-thirds of those take clerical jobs and the rest a range of other lower-skilled work. Women managers in retail, restaurants or salons are the worst affected, almost half giving up their managerial responsibilities to become sales assistants, hairdressers or something similar.

Even in teaching and nursing, generally considered to be careers that are sympathetic to part-time work, nearly one in ten quit for lower-skilled jobs. The study's authors concluded that: 'The one-and-a-half breadwinner model is not doing well by the more highly qualified among Britain's mothers ... the low quality of many part-time jobs means that women are paying the price of reconciling work and family.'

Deciding to join the mummy track isn't always a bad choice. Often women who make it have weighed up their decision carefully and can defend it robustly on the grounds that some sacrifice is acceptable if it allows them to be fulfilled mothers.

Once Beverly began to recover from her post-natal depression she also became slowly aware that continuing work as a research scientist, even though she had a PhD in immunology, felt unrealistic: 'Science is very output-orientated so you're judged on what you've got for your research, what results you get out of your lab and how many papers you publish. If I did it part-time I could probably tread water for a while but I wouldn't be getting anywhere, and you do need to be quite committed to getting your own lab.

'I was working with cells and you have to be in at weekends to feed them and wait until the cells are ready, then you have to work your life around your experiments and I didn't feel like I could be the parent I wanted to be and do that at the same time. When I was a post-doc student and I was pregnant, I saw other people drop their children off at 7.30 and pick them up at 7.30 and, you know, at the time I thought that was fine, but looking back, they really didn't have that much time with their kids and it must have been exhausting.

'But I did want to go back to work. I enjoyed being at home with my daughter but I also wanted something of my own, something to talk about once I felt my confidence come back a little bit. That was a big issue, thinking "Can I go back into the workplace?" It was quite scary.'

After searching through hundreds of job advertisements and specialist publications she came across an ad asking for someone with a scientific background to write review manuscripts, edit papers, and proofread manuscripts. She got the job, and was hired on a freelance basis which allowed her to work from home, apart from the odd visit to the university campus where her employer was based, to discuss their next project.

'I used to do the work when my daughter went to bed, so I was working really late. Just for the fun really, to get my brain working. I think that was the job that really boosted my confidence because I'd written my own papers but I'd never really written full review papers. I really enjoyed it and got something out of the work as well as a big lift when the papers were published.

'It got me back in the workplace and gave me the courage I needed to start looking at editors' positions, but they were all full-time so I just scoured the web for other things related to science that I could do part-time, and I came across the job I have now as a research administrator.'

Her two-and-a-half-day week is responsible and fulfilling. She works with academics trying to increase research income and also supporting them with their grant writing, an important role that involves financial management and record-keeping.

Perhaps more importantly, the new job allowed her another period of maternity leave. 'I got pregnant again quite quickly, which wasn't planned, and was only there for about a year and three months when I went on leave, but my employers were very good, very flexible and it was nice knowing I had a job to go back to.

'It was so different to the last time. I was a bit nervous coming back because I had been away so long but I soon got into the job again and didn't feel that complete drop of confidence as acutely because I had something to go back to and I knew the job.'

Should she feel resentful about being 'occupationally down-graded'? Having a PhD makes her part of the highly educated elite and may not be essential for her new job but any regrets she has are more than balanced, in her view, by the benefits of time spent with her children and lack of stress.

'I know it's not what I'm trained to do and obviously my first love would be science, you know to get down to the nitty-gritty and be at the bench, that's what I really like, but I don't feel I could do what I want at home, and then still do well at that too. I like to be able to do whatever job I am doing well, and I really don't think that I could give science my all and still have what I have at home. It does bother me, of course it does, but also I'm getting something else out of it, my family life and my children and having time to spend with them.'

Some surveys suggest that women are most satisfied with their jobs if they work less than fifteen hours a week once they have children and that the least happy women are those without a job. It may be that even though there is occupational downgrading, finding the right part-time job can be a zero sum game in which personal satisfaction as a mother balances the loss of income or professional standing. But what does happen to those women who, for entirely understandable reasons, give up full-time jobs and stimulating careers once they become mothers but don't manage to find that personal balance, possibly drifting from one unsatisfactory part-time job to another, then want to return to work later, maybe after their youngest child has started primary school, but find that they can't?

If they are supported by husbands or partners and are not claiming benefit they don't appear on unemployment statistics. Their wish to work flexibly may not 'fit' the jobs offered by traditional recruitment agencies, nor do they feature much as a political priority since they don't cost the taxpayer anything. The Office of National Statistics estimates that there are 4.7 million 'economically inactive' women of working age. A quarter of these would like to be working and around half a million of these want to work but cite family reasons for why they can't.

Many may be women who are less fulfilled than they might otherwise be, especially if they have lost confidence and skills, have no experience of paid childcare and above all have lost clarity about what their ambitions might be as their children grow older. They may have reached that point in a process as gradual and imperceptible as the one which takes their friends and neighbours into entirely new fulfilling careers or businesses. Their situation is likely to be the result of small steps *away* from work and new qualifications rather than towards them.

Hannah had a challenging, busy and glamorous job in the fashion industry before she had her children. But she felt it would be impossible to continue after they were born because of the travelling and the late nights it entailed.

The transition into a stay-at-home mum in the London suburbs took ten years. Now what she describes as her 'lazy, floaty life' sounds like the one every working mother periodically dreams of. Fully supported by her husband, she plays tennis, does yoga, takes time over the shopping in the middle of the day, rather than doing it at seven in the evening on the way home from work and definitely doesn't do her ironing at midnight. Yet it doesn't feel quite right.

'I had a languages degree so when my first baby was little I did a post-graduate translation diploma. I thought I would start on a new career path and become a translator but almost as soon as I got the diploma, my partner got posted abroad and so we moved away for five years which put a halt to me working.

'When we got back, I got some regular work but I found it terribly isolating. I didn't have childcare because I was on a long translation project which didn't require deadlines so I just wove it in and out of the children's needs. But I missed the social contact and any sort of feedback, so it just became a bit of a grind and not very satisfying.'

The social environment at her children's school also played a part in her lengthy detachment from work. 'There were a lot of non-working mothers there. I didn't feel they were judging me at all, but they are a very lively, vibrant group of women who had lots of money and were active in the PTA. I always felt I should be at my desk working but when my last big translation project came to an end, we moved house and I just started to enjoy doing voluntary work at the school, at our church and, more recently, at a museum and I slipped out of work altogether.

'It was funny because when I was at the museum I very much enjoyed being in a workplace, going out wearing different clothes and mixing with people who had a salary and some who had no children. I also liked the small amount of responsibility but at the same time I got slightly addicted to my flexible time. I didn't like to let them down but equally I liked the fact that the work was voluntary and I wasn't accountable. That made me feel more confident in a way and I thought that going for a paid job would have taken away my confidence.'

But even with a life that she acknowledges is highly privileged, the niggling desire to do something more is still there. 'I sometimes think other people must be looking at my life and thinking I should resent the fact that I have a degree and don't work. I don't feel resentful because they are my choices.

'But I do get frustrated sometimes. I do need to feed my brain with something and I feel envious that some of my friends have done incredibly well with these senior positions and also have children, although I have noticed that they usually have armies of childcare, or husbands who work flexible hours. My husband has really inflexible working hours and is a bit of a workaholic – he doesn't know how to do shorter hours. That is not the way it has ever been in my house, which has played a part in where I am now.'

The barriers to getting back into work after a long absence are never straightforward and often start with deep-seated anxieties about how to compete in a rapidly changing workplace after years of lost work experience. For Hannah, lack of confidence started with her worries about functioning in a modern high-tech office.

'It is the huge change in technology that frightens me and my skills deficit in that area. I left the workplace at a time when you would hand over the computer work to someone else to do in a separate room, no one had a computer on their desk. I think a lot of women who would like to go back to work feel secretly frightened of confronting the way it works now.'

Courses for IT beginners, or more advanced learners, are now widely available in a variety of settings through private providers and local authority adult and community education and can also be accessed through the Internet. But it is one thing to do the course, quite another to put it into practice. 'They are great while you are doing them but if you are not using it in the workplace then you can drop skills again so easily,' explains Hannah. 'And for me the next-biggest mental leap is committing to something on a long-term basis, to so many days a week, signing on the dotted line and changing my life.'

Making that psychological leap from wanting a job to actually getting one may be a hurdle that involves unpicking a jumble of practical and emotional issues. Domestic routines may need to be changed; some comfortable, well-worn habits will be left behind, afternoons ambling home from school with the children, morning coffee with your friends, taking long summer holidays. Workaholic partners who have never shared the domestic burden might require a shake-up and have to accept that they will need to do more, even if it is only childcare.

Hannah says she doesn't worry so much about the effect on the children of going back to work. 'They are older, more independent and less needy. The problem is with me because I would feel that I wasn't in control of their home help. I think to an extent I can be quite controlling and I want to do mothering really well. I think a lot of us get too attached to being there for our children and worry, maybe unnecessarily, about what would happen without us if they get ill or need someone to help out on a school trip when in fact they would easily survive.'

Signing on the dotted line for a new job after a long absence is a huge commitment – one that may not be easy to walk away from quickly. And it isn't just the immediate family who will feel it; friends and other relatives will have become used to your routine as much as you have and a decision to return to work will affect them too. But carrying an apprehensive family along with you may pale into insignificance against overcoming the most common legacy of years out of work: loss of self-esteem and fear of failure.

'I think it would feel horrible to fail at a job at this age and even worse if it is a job that isn't even that hard,' says Hannah. 'So I go around in circles.'

Karen Mattison's experience as a young working mother led her to set up her own social enterprise, Women Like Us, which combines finding women high-quality part-time jobs with coaching advice and is aimed at helping women who feel they are going round in circles and lack focus and confidence. She had a good job in the voluntary sector when her first two sons were born but felt she had stayed for too long simply because she had been able to negotiate her hours down to three days a week.

'I think I was quite bored and I wasn't developing my learning but it was local and flexible. I felt quite down about it, because I was just staying because it was handy. All the jobs that felt like a progression were full-time and I thought the children were too young for that. I had managed to get myself this three-day job and I couldn't work out how to move on.'

But work snowballed once she had made the decision to go freelance and work from home doing consultancy work for the voluntary sector. She found a business partner in a similar situation, they started to involve other women in pieces of work they couldn't do themselves and Karen started to spend much more time at the school gate, dropping off and picking up her children.

'I had never felt part of the school gate social scene. You do feel a bit out of it when you are working a lot but I gradually came to realise that the main topic of conversation among the women at the front gates was how to get a job they could fit around the kids. A constant refrain was "I was this before and I can't do that now". Perhaps their last child had just gone into reception and a lot of them were quite down about their prospects.

'Several of the other parents' stories were shocking. One woman had worked her way up to a good full-time job in the media but had packed in her career when her employers refused her request to go part-time when one of her children got ill and was in and out of hospital.

'When I met her she was working as a school meals supervisor because she wanted to do something that she could fit around the kids and couldn't find anything else. I thought it was absolutely ridiculous that she had all those skills and that experience. She was working as a dinner lady just so that she could get out of the house, but actually she had also taken the job of someone who didn't necessarily have the choices that she had got. I heard about a job that was perfect for her, persuaded her to go for it and she got it.'

'Then I met another woman who had been marketing manager in a big retail company and had also been refused the flexible working she wanted so she stopped work and had a third child. She was one of those women that you look at and think, "She is such a capable mother and so organised and confident," but I ended up having a similar conversation with her. She was desperate to get back to work but felt she had been out of the market for too long and had lost all her confidence. She seemed to be just looking for all the reasons she couldn't go back to work rather than looking for the ones that meant any employer would be lucky to have her. I coached her for an interview and she got the job.

'Everywhere we went we seemed to have the same conversations about loss of confidence and I even felt it myself after my third son was born. I remember walking into the office and thinking, "I can't do this." Even after only seven or eight months on maternity leave I felt exposed, lacking an edge, and thought if I felt like that going back after maternity leave to a secure job in an organisation that I was running, I can't imagine how it must feel to go back after five years, six years, to an office where all the technology has changed.

'But we realised that we also had to engage with employers. We knew that those elusive, quality, part-time jobs did exist and many employers knew that they wanted to find someone talented, experienced and flexible and that might well be a mum, but didn't know where to find them.'

Lack of clarity about what to do can be just as troubling as working out new practical arrangements and 'letting go' of old commitments. Former TV producer Louise feels she has drifted in and out of different, unstimulating jobs since she had her children.

'Before I had them I was working full-time in TV production but I didn't want to do that again because I wanted something I could do part-time, but that wasn't really good enough to warrant the whole nanny thing – and anyway I didn't like the thought of having someone else in the house – so I was trapped.

'I don't resent my kids at all but I do resent the situation. We were brought up to work and we were told to get out there and do it on our terms, but when I had my children I realised that it wasn't achievable. I've done admin for my other half because I couldn't *not* do anything for the sake of my sanity. For a while I tried starting up my own gardening design business but that proved very difficult. I have even done temping. I have never found anything that I could carry on into another career and most of the time I feel I am just searching for the right thing.

'I think that I have sacrificed my work life for my family life and my own needs in the workplace have undoubtedly been compromised and that is part of my struggle now, trying to get that back. I have had such fun with the kids but I do resent that I have never managed to make it work and my other half has. We are told all the time as women that we can do everything but that is just another pressure when all you really want is some clarity about the future, to be able to point yourself in the right direction.'

Finding time to think, if you are already performing an assortment of other roles that may include mother, partner, neighbour, friend, daughter, aunt and chief cook and bottle washer, is hard.

Hannah recognises that every time she starts feeling she might be able to start the process of 'finding the drive again' and move out of her comfort zone of tennis, voluntary work and yoga, something pops up and gets in the way.

'This comes up or that comes up, someone gets ill or there is a problem with one of the grandparents. Everything starts crowding in, I feel I am not doing my job properly as a mother and I go back to square one.'

Not having enough time is often the first line of defence women often use against making lifestyle changes. Women Like Us runs coaching sessions that initially just give women time to think about what they might want to do and what the necessary restrictions might be.

Are skills a problem? How important are part-time hours, flexible holiday arrangements, distance from home, level of pay, the provision of training and development opportunities, working in a team or alone? Does it matter to you that you are working in a company or organisation that you believe in, with certain ethical values, or will any employer do? Do you prefer working in a team or alone, in a big organisation and busy office or a smaller, quieter one? Are you prepared to take a risk on a job for which you aren't wholly qualified or prefer to stay safe, in a comfort zone using existing skills?

Many of these questions can be answered by making a list on the back of an envelope or by talking it through with friends. By the time Eve's children were approaching primary school she had already been made redundant from the publishing job that she'd had before she was pregnant, had a long period out of work, gone back because of financial pressures at home and then given up work again under the pressure of juggling all her roles with a child who was in and out of hospital. That made her clearer about what she did and didn't want to do once her children started full-time education.

'The first thing I realised was that it would have been much easier to try and stay in the job I had before I got pregnant. I didn't fight the redundancy but going back to work after a time at home is hard. It does lead to a confidence drop. I definitely suffered from one when I was at home with the boys. My confidence was really low about everything. I never thought I was a bad mother, but I felt marginalised as a woman and sort of below my peer group, especially other women with kids who had successfully gone back to work.

'However, because I had been back for one short period I knew that I preferred not being economically dependent on my husband. I also knew that I hated the travelling, and that the bits I thought I liked about work were the bits I couldn't actually do any more, like going to the pub and seeing my friends after work.

'But I also realised that I could go back and in fact once you do get back into the swing of things you remember a lot more than you think. My technical skills were absolutely fine and I actually found I could give my employers a lot of suggestions about how they could improve their working practices. I learnt that confidence does come back.'

Weighing up all the pros and cons helped her decide that going back to a job in publishing, her area of work experience, was not right because it would require a commute and the social benefits of a corporate job in a busy office were no longer relevant or accessible. She also still wanted to spend time with her children and remain part of the network of local mothers who had supported her over the years at home. Making the decision to start doing voluntary work in her children's primary school with a view to retraining as a primary school teacher, which would use her degree but allow her to have the holidays and some time after school, was a relief.

'My problem the second time around was that I just felt clouded and most of the mums I know who want to go back to work feel that way. What we all need is time out in the day to concentrate on ourselves and to realise that we aren't the only ones who have these concerns or experience this confusion.'

Tali, a petite, energetic former teacher who now liaises with the primary schools across London that link mothers to Women Like Us, says women get very isolated and negative about what they can and can't do.

'When they start talking to each other they realise they all feel the same way and that there is no barrier, apart from the one that they have created themselves,' she says. 'I gave up work when my youngest daughter was about two. I had childcare linked to the school but it was miles from where we lived. I used to leave at ten past, quarter past seven in the morning. The children would be crying and I would be trying to give my elder daughter food in the car and I just felt horribly guilty and found the whole lot too much. In the end I just thought I'm going to have a nervous breakdown. They were really really supportive at school but I just couldn't carry on. So I left work for a bit just to have a bit of time off to get my head straight.'

A complicated and traumatic third pregnancy, which resulted in her son being delivered early after she developed a liver malfunction, led to several years out of work. 'I think it psychologically took me longer to recover. I just felt the whole burden of what could have happened to him. But by the time he was coming up to about two and started going to a little nursery I suddenly got this feeling of despair that this was the rest of my life, because I couldn't work out how on earth to get back to work. I do love being a mum but I was getting bored. I needed to do something for myself.'

When the job at Women Like Us came up, Tali had got so out of touch with work that she had never even sent an email. 'The first time I got paid I just thought fantastic and went out to buy a pair of shoes! It was so exciting, I was working locally so didn't have to worry about travelling or childcare and it was great just to be contributing to the household purse again and to be with other people and I don't feel I have wasted my qualifications. I feel comfortable in schools because of my background but I have learnt to use my skills in different ways.'

A long period out of work can easily lead women to massively underestimate their skills. Men and women who are moving from one job to another in continuous employment are usually so well versed in the art of promotion and the jargon of recruitment that they often find people don't even question their ability to move onwards and upwards. Have you ever noticed how many men will look at a job advert and think immediately 'I can do that', whereas many women, especially if they have had a career break and lost work experience, will look at the same ad and think, 'I can't', even though they may have learned many new 'transferable' skills in their time out of paid employment.

Being a mother involves deadlines, multi-tasking, prioritising, meeting new people – whether the school gate mafia or new neighbours – tapping into long-lost creativity and emotional skills like anger management, encouragement and patience. Sometimes women don't realise how well equipped they are.

Even with a catering qualification behind her and ten years' experience as a cook employed in a variety of private-sector companies, Victoria's self-esteem was low after fifteen years at home raising her four children. She found it hard to contemplate what she might do, let alone how she would find the right job to match her children's needs. 'When a job came up in a local inner-city primary school running a cookery club and promoting healthy eating, my immediate thought was that I couldn't possibly get it,' she said.

But once she started to write down everything she had done in her life both in and out of work, much of which she didn't acknowledge as personal strengths, she became an outstanding candidate. Not only did she have her catering diploma but she had been volunteering in her children's own primary school and a local playgroup (which provided excellent references), her own daughter's successful battle against leukaemia had turned her into an expert and evangelist about healthy eating for children, and even her lifelong passion and knowledge about gardening gave her an edge over other candidates as the school was interested in linking its cookery club with what was going on in the school garden.

She got the job and recently featured in a film about the school's extracurricular activities and is now building up a specialism working with children on food and health issues. 'It was a bit difficult with my own children at first, they were quite horrified about the thought of me going back to work because they have got so used to me being around, but I can be at home before and after school and in the holidays. I now combine the job with working in another nursery, and some days I get three or four "I love you"s from the kids and so much pleasure out of helping some of them, who have no real understanding of where food comes from or how you can eat nutritiously but relatively cheaply.'

The network that led her to the job wasn't a professional one but a local one. Women may recognise the power of local networks for domestic help and support but overlook the fact that they may also be useful on the journey back to work.

The term 'networking' can seem off-putting, redolent of high-powered professional and social relationships which revolve around breakfast meetings, power lunches and drinks after work rather than book clubs, school associations or the local church. But all networking really means is getting in touch with people. Looking at job ads in newspapers or recruitment agencies can help to build confidence. 'I regularly look for jobs in the *Guardian*,' says Hannah, 'and occasionally I do see things that I think I could do, which gives me a nice butterfly feeling in my stomach that, yes, I could do that.' But local networks might be just as good a way of hearing about job opportunities that are family friendly.

Some estimates suggest that for every job advertised there may be over a thousand CVs in circulation. A significant proportion of jobs never get advertised, even though they may prove to be a much richer source of flexible or part-time work, but they may be available through local networks.

Dee's journey from a relatively unqualified mother of three into journalism and publishing started with her involvement in a local women's health centre and the networks that fanned out from there. 'I was about twenty-five. A combination of having my daughter young meant that I was mostly at home and rarely ventured out beyond a small area and a small circle of people. I started volunteering in the local women's health centre and then started to write their newsletter. That is how I found out about a literature development course at a local community centre and from there started to hear about careers in journalism. Eventually that took me on to the access course that led to my degree.

'While I was at college I was always busy working for the community centre. They invited me to edit special newsletters and special editions for children. I got to do some commissioning, some writing and more editing. I was always very busy looking for opportunities to do journalism for free and you know that gave me the experience that I needed so that before I even finished my degree I had got a job on a local newspaper.'

Networks or not, the thorny issue of the CV and job application can prove the last hurdle to leap over, especially if you have long career gaps to account for. Sally's self-esteem was at rock bottom after an eight-year career gap between giving up her job as a TV producer when she had the first of her three children and trying to re-enter the labour market. 'I was depressed, not working. I had gone from a very equal relationship with my husband to one that was very unequal and I didn't like being dependent.

'Two things saved me, one was becoming a school governor, the other was standing in a local council election which then led to me becoming a trustee of a local community centre and I also started doing some hospital radio broadcasting as a volunteer. I wasn't doing any paid work but I began to feel more confident and, more importantly, I was doing something that wasn't to do with the family.

'All the things I was doing involved campaigning, one way or another. I was gaining skills that I didn't have before, like being able to speak in public and to organise myself and other people. I ran a successful campaign for a school uniform at my children's primary school which was an interesting experience because the more well-off parents didn't want it and the poorer ones did and, even though I didn't get elected to the council, I began to realise that I was as good as all the people I was involved with who were working full-time. That also gave me the confidence to think I could go back to work.'

However, she knew that she had to manage the presentation of an eight-year career break when she started reapplying for jobs.

'I knew people were going to say to me "What did you do in those eight years after you left television?" and I still find that difficult to explain away. But I found an ad in a national paper for a job as campaigns manager for a national charity close to where I lived. It felt like the perfect job and I managed to write my career break into a narrative that started with my media experience and ended up with me being able to provide evidence that I had lots of experience of campaigning, which by then I did.'

Not all employers expect to see a timeline. In the end most want to hear about how an applicant's ability, competence and experience, even if they have been developed in a career break, can match what they want. A CV can be written as a list of skills with relevant evidence to back them up as easily as a list of jobs.

If you've got the confidence to do that, you will probably also have the guts to ask whether flexible or part-time work is possible, even if the job advert doesn't specify that. Making an immediate commitment to work full-time after a period at home could be too much of a leap. If your prospective employers want you enough they may agree, even though the law currently only offers the right to ask for flexible work to employees who have been in the post for twenty-six weeks.

'My daughter was only about five or six months old when I made the application to do a new job closer to home,' says Emma. 'I applied saying that I would only be available to work four days and asked if they would see me under those circumstances. The HR department was very lukewarm but they did give me a second interview. It was for a managerial position but the interview went well and they were happy to let me start four days a week which was good. Maybe that wouldn't have happened if someone else they wanted had been prepared to work full-time. But I think personnel departments have to follow the line that is in the job advertisement, so that's what they will tell you if you contact them in advance. But if you don't ask, you will never find out.'

Tessa took the same approach when applying for a new job closer to her family home in the Oxfordshire countryside after the family relocated from London. 'I had been at home for some time and had tried doing some writing but I found it really hard. Gradually I realised I liked going to work to meet people and I didn't want to sit in a village house all day. People would just pop round all the time and then couldn't understand why I wasn't free to just chat when I normally seemed to have lots of time. Half of me would be thinking I would much rather be having a gossip and then half the morning would be gone, so I knew I had to get back to a proper job outside.

'I started applying for jobs only to get to the interview stage and realise I actually wanted to work part-time. The first time I did it, I am afraid I waited until the interview was over before actually saying it, which was a bit of a horror. But the response was fine. In fact they told me that the person interviewed before me had asked exactly the same thing and they gave me the job. Now I wouldn't hesitate to ask.'

It may be easy to feel marginalised after a period at home with the children or in a job that doesn't match your aspirations. But it doesn't have to be a mummy track to oblivion. The early feminist Mary Wollstonecraft wrote that she didn't want women to have power over men 'but over themselves'. A long career break can feel disempowering and demoralising. But there is no rule that says being fulfilled by enjoying your children annuls past work experience. It may even enhance it.

Once Sally campaigned her way back into work after eight years of frustration that her once evenly balanced relationship had become hopelessly lopsided, she realised that her life was divided neatly in two parts.

'In part one I screwed up a bit. I had the children and let my husband become the power in the home, earn all the money and quietly move away from taking responsibility for anything. In part two I have regained my sense of equality. He now has to come home and make dinner for the kids.

'I don't just feel I am a better role model to them now. Anything is possible.'

Final Thoughts

When I was in the final stages of writing this book, I ran into a very senior politician at a party. An old friend and also a parent of young children, he asked me what I was working on. When I explained, his immediate reaction was, 'So what's your theory then?'

As I racked my brain to come up with a quick sound-bite answer, it dawned on me that I didn't have one. Understandably, politicians want simple, easily executed solutions to what are often intractable problems. But as the child and adolescent psychiatrist Sebastian Kraemer wisely points out in chapter 1, politicians can't know every baby, or every mother, father or family.

So if there is any conclusion at all, it is that no hard and fast rules apply. Every baby is different, some may find it relatively easy to be apart from their mothers, virtually wean themselves and settle quickly with new carers. But others suffer painful and heart-wrenching separation anxiety. Some mothers find being parted from their babies harder than friends and colleagues, who may love their children no less, but are mentally and physically equipped to go back more swiftly to working outside the home.

What is more, you will never really know how motherhood takes you until you are doing it. I certainly never anticipated that, within nine months of giving birth, I would give up the job I had worked hard to get and progressed in for seven years. Unlike Angela, the science graduate with a stimulating job in industry, who became overwhelmed by resentment of her baby daughter's nanny, I didn't mind the thought of my son bonding with someone else. I just wanted to spend more time with him myself and couldn't see the point of having a child I never saw. I also soon became ground down by the 'unforgiving minute', the mad dash to the supermarket on the way home from work and the fact that weekends became a series of dreary chores. I never really bought the idea of 'quality time'. Any extra time, quality or not, would have suited me more than none at all.

But the desire to distil arguments like should mothers work, or how should they work, into simply theories is dangerous because value judgements become implicit in the answers. It is undoubtedly the case that allowing mothers, and fathers, more time at home with their babies in the first year is welcome. But does that mean that mothers who choose to go back to work earlier are bad mothers who risk damaging their children's longer-term well-being?

When Amelia decided not to take her full leave entitlement, partly because she wanted to avoid restarting work at the time when the risk of her daughter experiencing separation anxiety increased, she was conscious that it gave her a good reason to explain her decision to others.

Like it or not, once we set out a norm for how we expect mothers to behave, anyone who deviates from it runs the risk of being judged abnormal in some way. There is no doubt that some eyebrows will be raised over Sangita's decision to return to work when her baby son was four months old, leaving him in a nursery four days a week and battling with staff who insisted he should be taken home when he was ill, rather than given Calpol and kept there as his mother suggested. Likewise, the decisions other women make to give up work completely and be 'stay-at-home' mums can attract equal scorn and suspicion among friends and colleagues who have made a decision to keep working. Given that 70 per cent of mothers do now work, theirs might be the harder choice to justify.

Trying to settle on a 'right' or a 'wrong' way to combine work and family is a pointless exercise, rather like judging a two-parent family to be automatically superior to a lone parent one. Interestingly, both judgements subliminally suggest that women, rather than men, are the culprits. Unless we can go into every individual home, understand the quality of the relationships between every parent and every child, as well as grasping the domestic economics, the personal and intellectual stimulation that work can bring and which *may* make many women better mothers, none of us is in a position to say that another woman's choices are more or less valid than our own.

So much of the argument about working mothers revolves around the mother and baby relationship, as if life froze at this point, children never grew up and women simply carried on doing the same jobs they always did. But being separated from your baby is only the first stage in a lifetime of juggling emotions and practical arrangements, which as we have seen throughout this book can prove to be more complicated than the initial ups and downs of those early months and years.

Similarly, the ease with which relationships with colleagues, employers, husbands and partners coexist with or disrupt the pleasure and pain of being a parent also defies rules and regulations.

It may be possible to go back to the same job and find that nothing has changed; that colleagues don't think you have divided loyalties, or that you are always trying to skive off early to be with the kids. Your employers may give you credit for being an even better multitasker and manager of time than you were before your maternity leave. Who knows, you may even find yourself in the same situation as Caitlin, the senior sales manager who was the first person in her organisation to ask for flexible working. She then threatened legal action when she was offered it in a less prestigious job, and managed to keep her pay status and company car entitlement on a four-day week.

But we would be kidding ourselves if we thought that such auspicious circumstances awaited every newly returning mother. It is equally possible that colleagues will be waiting to seize on your every mistake, making it clear that, to them, a part-time job means a part-time commitment. Jane, a senior newspaper executive who threw in the towel, went off and eventually started her own business after she discovered that her workmates and former friends were even laying bets about how long she would last in the job.

It may be that employers are neither positive nor negative, but that the multiple burden of work, providing financial and emotional support to the family, doing the domestic chores and organising childcare, conspires to create a tipping point.

Gill gave up her clerical job in the City and her relationship with her daughter's father when all these, combined with a long commute, led her to the conclusion that she was living a 'rat on a wheel existence'. In many such circumstances, change may become inevitable. Gill became a lone parent, went back to college and ended up retraining as a solicitor in her thirties.

Women do have much more changeable working patterns than their partners, husbands and male colleagues. They often become the primary carers and the secondary earners once they have children. Successive periods of maternity leave can interrupt work experience and put a strain on existing relationships with employers who may, subconsciously or not, have a changed view of a female employee with a family.

Hard and fast rules become even harder as children grow up. Childcare and work schedules that seem fine for an infant or toddler may prove impractical for school-age children or a different job. After giving up her career in journalism to start her own PR company, Jane relied heavily on schools which provided after-school clubs. But for Caitlin, having kept a high-status job in business, neither a childminder nor a play centre provided the solution. She ended up hiring a nanny and paying more for her childcare than she did before the children started school, in order to achieve the flexibility required by the combination of a demanding job and her daughters' varied out-of-school interests.

Children who settle easily into nursery and primary school may become unfamiliar aliens in their teens. Every woman I spoke to with older children stressed the difficulties of finding the right sort of care for young adolescents. Liz, the Welsh lawyer who took a career break when her children were starting secondary school, describes the moment she knew she couldn't carry on working as an 'epiphany'. This was triggered by one disrupted night spent with two children throwing up – before a day in which she and her husband both had heavy professional commitments. She was lucky to have the financial back-up that enabled her to make that decision. Others, like Dee, didn't have that luxury. She worked and got a degree throughout her son's troubled primary and secondary school years but also devoted all her other waking hours to supporting him and two other older children through GCSEs and A levels and eventually started her own magazine to help other parents. Even the mothers I met who had children in late primary school were starting to worry about the next five or six years, especially if they lived in areas where their children faced long journeys to and from school.

But even if there isn't a single theory about how women can and should manage work and family, there are several themes that recur in any conversations on this subject whether you speak to women who have just given birth, have juggled for ten years or more, have been out of the workplace, who are highly qualified, have left school at sixteen, are in full- or part-time work. The common themes revolve around income, flexibility, personal identity, roles, children and families.

It is hard not to have some sympathy with the politicians, dealing with the big social- and public-spending issues rather than the individual and the personal. But too often the issue of women's work is presented either in the context of the contribution it might make to the economy generally, or the knock-on effect it will have on the benefit system.

But most women don't walk around thinking they must get a job or continue working to boost the nation's gross national product, pay more taxes, or to help cut the welfare budget. However varied their choices may be, this decision is invariably made on the basis of what is right for them and best for their family. Policies relating to working mothers need to recognise that.

If we do think 'children and family first', several things become clear. Whether or not women, or indeed men, want to take four or fourteen months off work, maternity leave should be extended, better-funded and, in the later stages, more readily shared with fathers. The early bond between mother and baby is the foundation on which later relationships, good mental health, social behaviour and achievement are built. That doesn't mean that in the course of the first year, other carers – and particularly fathers – can't form equally strong relationships with infants or that women shouldn't leave their babies and go back to work. There is not enough honesty about the fact that being alone at home all day with a small baby can be demoralising and lonely, especially for women who have no one else to share the care with, and a depressed mother can be at home but still find it hard to bond with her baby.

But it does mean that those vital early months should be protected for women who want to wait until they and their babies are ready to be apart from each other. Too many women who don't benefit from good occupational maternity-leave schemes and who aren't supported by another working parent still need to return to work before they or their children are ready. This isn't about judging mothers, but about acknowledging that there may be a personal cost to them and their baby if they aren't able to make the choices that are right for them, choices another mother might be able to make freely. The argument that maternity pay should be raised to at least minimum wage levels deserves more serious and urgent attention.

Families also need access to more good-quality, affordable childcare. The transition back to work can be made or broken by finding the right care, whether it is a nursery, a childminder, a nanny or a mixture of formal and informal care such as friends, neigh-bours and grandparents. It is no coincidence that so many women use the word 'nightmare' to describe the process of finding the right care for their children, whether they are small babies or teenagers. Deciding to whom you should entrust what Julia, a mother on a relatively low income, described as 'her most precious possession', can be fraught with emotion and doubt.

Her experience of living through the news that her son's nursery was failing is one that most working parents would rather avoid. Mothers do have more choice and information than ever before about the people who look after their babies and their older children and there are many more good and outstanding nurseries, loving responsive nannies and childminders than there were twenty years ago.

But a small minority – 4 per cent – of nurseries and childminders have been judged not good enough, and that is 4 per cent too many. These statistics are often used to fuel the often overblown claims that 'non-maternal care' is by definition damaging, and give oxygen to the attachment theorists and anti-childcare fanatics who one suspects might really prefer women to just go back into the home and forget about jobs or careers.

It is not the case that every child who goes into a nursery will turn into a deviant or 'yob'. A small proportion of children put into day care at a very young age do show some signs of challenging behaviour, but that might have happened even if they had been at home in the same period, and often that phase passes. Much of the evidence about the effects of day care comes from the USA, where mothers' maternity rights are paltry and many babies attend full- or part-time day care from the age of six weeks.

Many women in the UK now manage to take around five or six months' maternity leave, and those who can afford it take even longer, so the context is very different. Most of the women interviewed for this book were satisfied that their children had benefitted from a decent period of care at home with one or other of their parents. This made the change to being looked after by someone else relatively painless, especially if the parents were able to achieve some degree of flexibility at work and the carer was consistent, sensitive and well trained.

However, moving towards a situation where childcare is more heavily subsidised by the state, and all childcare workers are required to have higher-level qualifications – in some Nordic countries they are required to have a Masters degree – would clearly eliminate the element of doubt that still exists in the eyes of some mothers. Much of the anxiety can be taken out of the process of returning to work if your children are visibly happy and settled while you are away.

The right to ask for flexible work is still in its infancy and, though it is still working patchily, has opened up an expectation that the office, factory, restaurant or shop can change. Women, and some men, are having conversations with their employers that they probably wouldn't have dared to entertain twenty or thirty years ago. Several women featured in this book even asked to work flexibly at interviews for full-time jobs – and got the jobs.

But the right to ask is a long way from the right to choose working patterns that fit in with your family life. Employers can still refuse a request. If we accept that one-size-fits-all arrangements won't work for every family then it is in the employers' interest to deliver tailor-made solutions that are likely to benefit both parties; the employer retains well-trained, happy staff and the staff themselves are motivated and in a position to give their best to the company. Unfortunately, despite several research studies that prove the case for flexible work, too many employers are still not prepared to contemplate managing staff in more innovative ways, creating a shortage of quality, part-time jobs in senior or management positions. Ideally, this should change and the right to flexible working should quickly be extended to include the parents of older children, to allow them to accommodate potential problems that the onset of adolescence can bring. It should also be available to all parents, both mothers and fathers, whether or not they have been in their job for six months, and its very existence should be robustly defended, especially at a time of economic downturn when some of the employers' organisations will argue that it is an unnecessary regulation.

What is needed is for more men to start demanding flexible or part-time work and for them to challenge some of the assumptions that still exist about men's position in the workplace, in particular that only long hours equate with masculinity, that wanting to spend time with your children is somehow soft or that a part-time job will result in full-time colleagues having to shoulder a greater load. Evidence from other countries that have tried to nudge more fathers into sharing parental leave may not always be encouraging. But if more men did start to take significant time off in the first year of their children's lives, possibly through making extra leave conditional on the father's uptake, it might start to shift that domestic burden. It might also, and it is a big 'might', start to change the culture of many workplaces where men still feel reluctant to ask for more flexibility, or employers are still resistant to granting it.

Too many women still suffer negative assumptions from their employers and colleagues about the contribution they can make at work once they have had children. While they may in theory be protected by the law against discrimination arising from their changed circumstances, proving sex discrimination is notoriously difficult and almost impossible without outside financial support. The two women interviewed for this book who had challenged poor employment practices at work were only able to do so because they were backed by their trade unions. Many women only find out how much they might have benefitted from being a union member when it is too late.

But neither trade unions nor employment law can fully protect women from the now well-documented gradual slide down the pay and promotion ladder that often follows a period of intermittent work and one or more chunks of maternity leave. Call it what you like, occupational downgrading … the mummy track … the hidden brain drain; it is a vicious cycle that many of us face, especially if we opt for part-time or flexible work.

The Oxford sociologist Professor Jonathan Gershuny's description of this as a modern-day perversion of the Cinderella fairy tale – in which Allerednic doesn't start in the scullery and end up with the prince, but instead starts with her on a professional pinnacle and then descends to the drudgery of doing two jobs, at home and work, while falling behind in status and pay – has no happy ending. As the pressure of being a dual-earner family starts to bite, the mother cuts back or gives up working altogether, losing skills, confidence and self-esteem over a longer period, which makes a viable return to the labour market, once her children are older, appear impossible.

But the final question we must ask is what do women want? The idea that we have somehow got tired with juggling, realise we can't have it all, would rather be at home with the children or feel we *should* be at home with the children, is gathering slow and rather worrying momentum. There is a grain of truth there. Having it all has often meant doing it all; phrases like 'holding it all together', 'keeping my head above water' and 'struggling' were heard in many of the conversations I had with interviewees, friends and acquaintances while researching this book.

Being a working mother can be hellish. We can all list the low points: walking out the door on a screaming, fractious baby, or walking back in to one, doing your ironing at midnight, entertaining the nagging suspicion that your stay-at-home neighbour, or the rest of the playground mafia, are better, more satisfied mothers than you, having to find emergency childcare, or being at work and trying to pin down a missing teenager who should be at home.

Most of us probably would like to be at home with the children more and often feel we should be, not least because of the bucketloads of blame that are lined up for working mothers, who are – according to a section of the media – variously responsible for everything from childhood obesity and high divorce rates to poor performance in school and antisocial behaviour. Working fathers are rarely implicated in these.

However, that doesn't mean that we don't want, or need, to work too. All the women interviewed for this book talked about how much it meant to them to have a job outside the home. The reasons they gave were usually a variation on the same theme. Working, whether full-time or part-time, gave them self-respect, a degree of independence (especially financial), a chance to use their brains in a different way and to feel stimulated by and interested in something other than their families which, incidentally, is not a crime.

Above all, women's personal identities were very much bound up with their sense of themselves as independent working people, as well as mothers. The women who had stopped work altogether were doubly conflicted about that, aware that they had given something up that might be irretrievable. We strive so hard now to instil in our daughters the idea that they can and should achieve as well as if not better than boys, proceed to higher education, get jobs and make something of their lives. It is completely perverse that so much ambivalence still exists about whether they should continue to fulfil that potential once they have children.

There may not be a simple 'theory' that will put all this right, but there is a big political argument. It is about fairness, equality, children, families and personal fulfilment. The politician who ignores this does so at his, or her, peril.

APPENDIX 1

Bibliography

Barrett, Helen, *Attachment and the Perils of Parenting*, National Family & Parenting Institute 2006

BBC News, 'Mothers care "best" for children', BBC News website, 3 October 2005, www.bbc.co.uk

Beckford, Martin, 'Mothers find it harder than ever to juggle work and family life', *Telegraph*, 6 August 2008

Belsky, Jay, 'Major Findings from the NICHD Study of Early Child Care', Institute for the Study of Children, Families and Social Issues, www.iscfsi.bbk.ac.uk

Belsky, Jay, Vandell, Deborah Lowe, Burchinal, Margaret, Clarke-Stewart, K. Alison, McCartney, Kathleen & Owen, Margaret Tresch, 'Are there long term effects of Early Child Care?', *Child Development*, 78, April 2007

Benn, Melissa, 'When did you last see your husband?', *Guardian*, 9 April 2005

Benn, Melissa, *Madonna and Child: Politics of Modern Motherhood*, Jonathan Cape 1998

Berthoud, Richard & Gershuny, Jonathan, eds., *Seven Years in the Lives of British Families*, Policy Press 2000

Booth, Alison & van Ours, Jan, 'Job Satisfaction, Family Life and Happiness: The Part Time Work Puzzle', *Economic Journal*, 118, February 2008

Boswell, Sophie, *Understanding Your Baby*, Jessica Kingsley 2004

Brewer, Nicola, 'Developing The Ties That Bind Fairness For All', Speech at the Public Policy Exchange Conference 2008, www.equalityhumanrights.com

Bunting, Madeleine, 'Nursery Tales', *Guardian*, 8 July 2004

Coleman, John C. & Hendry, Leo B., *The Nature of Adolescence*, Routledge 1999

Connolly, Sara & Gregory, Mary, 'Moving Down: Women's Part-time work and Occupational Change in Britain 1991–2001', *Economic Journal*, 118, February 2008

Cranfield School of Management, 'Flexible Work and Performance', Working Families 2008

Crompton, Rosemary, & Lyonette, Clare, 'Work-life "balance" in Europe', Genet Working Paper no 10, www.genet.ac.uk

Daycare Trust, 'Childcare Costs Survey 2008', Daycare Trust website www.daycaretrust.org.uk

Daycare Trust, 'Childcare Nation', Daycare Trust website www.daycaretrust.org.uk

Daycare Trust, 'Listening to Children about Childcare', Daycare Trust website www.daycaretrust.org.uk

Department for Business Enterprise and Regulatory Reform website www.berr.gov.uk

Department of Work and Pensions 'Maternity Rights and Mothers Employment Decisions 19 June 2008', Department of Work and Pensions website www.dwp.gov.uk

Desforges, Charles & Abouchaar, Albert, 'The Impact of Parental Involvement on Children's Education', Department for Education and Skills 2003, www.dcsf.gov.uk

Directgov website www.direct.gov.uk

Early Years Commission, 'The Next Generation', The Centre for Social Justice 2008, www.centreforsocialjustice.org.uk

Enterprising Women website www.enterprising-women.org

Equal Opportunities Commission, 'Dads and their babies: a household analysis', EOC Working Papers 2006, www.equalityhuman rights.com

Equal Opportunities Commission, 'Dads and their babies: the mothers' perspective', EOC Working Papers 2005, www.equalityhumanrights.com

Equal Opportunities Commission, 'Shared caring: bringing fathers into the frame', EOC Working Papers 2005, www.equalityhuman rights.com

Equalities and Human Rights Commission, 'The Gender Agenda: The Unfinished Revolution', Equalities and Human Rights Commission, www.equalityhumanrights.com

Everywoman website www.everywoman.com

FCCC website www.familieschildrenchildcare.org

Figes, Kate, *Life After Birth*, Virago Press 2008

Figes, Kate, *The Terrible Teens: What Every Parent Needs to Know*, Penguin 2004

Gatrell, Caroline, *Hard Labour. The Sociology of Parenthood*, Open University Press 2004

Gerhardt, Sue, *Why Love Matters: How Affection Shapes a Baby's Brain*, Routledge 2004

Gershuny, Jonathan, 'The Work Life Balance and the new Political Economy of Time', The Downing Street Millennium Lecture, 27 January 1999

Gershuny, Jonathan, Bitman, Michael & Brice, John, 'Exit, Voice and Suffering: Do Couples Adapt to Changing Employment Patterns?', *Journal of Marriage and Family*, 67, August 2005

Graham, Philip, *The End of Adolescence: Exposing the Myths About the Teenage Years*, Oxford University Press 2004

Gregg, Paul, Washbrook, Elizabeth, Propper, Carol & Burgess, Simon, 'The Effects of a Mother's Return to Work Decision on Child Development in the UK', *Economic Journal*, 115, February 2005

Gupta, Nabanita Datta, Smith, Nina, & Verner, Mette, 'A Model to Aspire to? Experiences from the Nordic countries on Parental Leave Schemes', Aarhus School of Business

Hakim, Catherine, *Key Issues in Women's Work*, Routledge-Cavendish 2004

Health and Safety for New and Expectant Mothers website www.hse.gov.uk/mothers

Hilpern, Kate, 'Well, why haven't my shirts been ironed?', *Guardian*, 2 February 2008

Houston, D.M. & Marks, G., 'Working, Caring and Sharing: Work Life Dilemmas in Early Motherhood' in Houston, D.M., (ed), *Work Life Balance in the Twenty First Century*, Palgrave Macmillan 2005

Institute of Education, 'The Effective Provision of Pre School Education Project', Institute of Education 2003, www.ioe.ac.uk

James, Oliver, *Affluenza*, Vermilion 2007

Johnson, Rebecca, 'Michelle Obama Interview: I'm nothing special', *Telegraph Magazine*, 26 July 2008

Kraemer, Sebastian, 'Parenting Yesterday Today and Tomorrow' in Dwidvedi, K.N, ed, *Enhancing Parenting Skills*, Wiley 1997

Lea, Ruth, 'Work Life Balance Revisited', IOD website www.iod.co.uk

Leach, Penelope, *Your Baby and Child*, Dorling Kindersley 2003

Learndirect website www.learndirect.co.uk

Manning, Alan & Petrongolo, Barbara, 'The Part Time Pay Penalty', *Economic Journal*, 118, February 2008

Marrin, Minette, 'Pushing mothers back to work is wrong', *Sunday Times*, 2 September 2007

Maushart, Susan, *Wifework: What Marriage Really Means for Women*, Bloomsbury Publishing 2003

Mumsnet website www.mumsnet.com

Nannyshare website www.nannyshare.co.uk

National Institute of Child Health and Human Development, 'Study of Early Child Care and Youth Development', National Institute of Child Health and Human Development, secc.rti.org

National Network for Childcare website www.nncc.org

Netmums website www.netmums.com

Newpin services, Family Action website www.family-action.org.uk

NHS Breastfeeding website www.breastfeeding.nhs.uk

O'Grady, Frances & Wakefield, Heather, *Women, Work and Maternity: The Inside Story*, The Maternity Alliance 1989

Ofsted, 'Leading to Excellence', Ofsted website www.ofsted.gov.uk

OXPIP (Oxford Parent Infant Project) website oxpip.org.uk

Parker, Rozsika, *Torn in Two: Maternal Ambivalence*, Virago Press 2005

Paull, Gillian, 'Children and Women's Hours of Work', *Economic Journal*, 118, February 2008

Prowess website www.prowess.org.uk

Roberts, Elizabeth, *A Woman's Place. An Oral History of Working Class Women 1890–1940*, Wiley Blackwell 1995

Roberts, Elizabeth, *Women's Work 1840–1940*, Cambridge University Press 1995

Scott, Jacqueline, Dex, Shirley, Joshi, Heather, *Women and Employment. Changing Lives and New Challenges*, Edward Elgar Publishing 2008

SEED Networking for Women website www.seednetworkingfor women.com

Sharpe, Pamela, *Adapting to Capitalism: Working Women in the English Economy 1700–1850*, Palgrave Macmillan 2000

Sharpe, Pamela, *Women's Work. The English Experience 1650–1914*, Hodder Arnold 1998

Sure Start website www.surestart.gov.uk

The Work Foundation website www.theworkfoundation.com

Thomson, Rachel & Kehily, Mary Jane, 'The Making of Modern Motherhood', ESRC Identities and Social Action, www.identities. org.uk

Tinies website www.tinies.com

UK Statistics Authority website www.statistics.gov.uk

Vincent, Carol & Ball, Stephen, *Childcare Choice and Class Practices: Middle-class parents and their children*, Routledge 2006

W M Women's Business Centre website www.wmwomensbusinesscentre.com

Warner, Judith, *Perfect Madness: Motherhood in the Age of Anxiety*, Vermilion 2006

Williams, Fiona, *Rethinking Families*, Calouste Gulbenkian Foundation 2004

Women and Work Commission, 'Shaping a Fairer Future', Women and Work Commission 2006

Women and Work Commission, 'Towards a Fairer Future: Implementing the Women and Work Commission Recommendations', Department of Communities and Local Government, April 2007

Women Like US website www.womenlikeus.org.uk

Working Families website www.workingfamilies.org.uk

Useful Resources

Books

Figes, Kate, *Life After Birth*, Virago Press 2008

Figes, Kate, *The Terrible Teens: What Every Parent Needs to Know*, Penguin 2004

Leach, Penelope, *Your Baby and Child*, Dorling Kindersley 2003

Maushart, Susan, *Wifework: What Marriage Really Means for Women*, Bloomsbury Publishing 2003

Organisations

Childcare Vouchers

Providers of childcare vouchers, a cost effective way for companies to attract and retain talented staff.

www.childcarevouchers.co.uk

Daycare Trust

A charity promoting high-quality affordable childcare. They offer advice to parents seeking the best arrangements for their family and employers looking to set up schemes for their employees.

www.daycaretrust.org

Directgov
Provides access to information on all government services, including child benefits and trust funds, maternity and paternity rights in the workplace and schools.
www.direct.gov.uk

Equality and Human Rights Commission
An independent statutory body established to help eliminate discrimination, reduce inequality, protect human rights and to build good relations, and to ensure that everyone has a fair chance to participate in society.
www.equalityhumanrights.com

HM Revenue and Customs
The childcare page provides links to information about tax and National Insurance contributions on employer-supported childcare and other related government departments.
www.hmrc.gov.uk/childcare

Learndirect
Flexible learning courses that can be taken online at home or at a local centre.
www.learndirect.co.uk

Mumsnet
Parenting advice site.
www.mumsnet.com

Netmums
Parenting advice site.
www.netmums.com

Raisingkids
Parenting advice site.
www.raisingkids.co.uk

Sure Start
A government programme which aims to increase the availability of childcare, improve health and emotional development for young children and support parents in their aspirations towards employment.
www.surestart.gov.uk

TUC (Trades Union Congress)
The TUC has fifty-eight affiliated unions representing nearly seven million working people from all walks of life. They campaign for a fair deal at work and for social justice at home and abroad.
www.tuc.org.uk

Women Like Us
Women Like Us helps women with children find work they can fit around their families and helps employers to recruit flexible, talented staff. They offer coaching and consultancy services, specialising in flexible working.
www.womenlikeus.org.uk

Working Families
Offers the most comprehensive guidance on flexible working and how to deal with other working parent employment issues.
www.workingfamilies.org.uk

Index

Some of the proceeds from the sale of this book will be paid to the social enterprise Women Like Us.